THE VIKINGS

RAIDERS, EXPLORERS AND SEAFARING WARRIORS

By Lance Hightower

CW01583523

Copyright 2016 by Lance Hightower

Published by Make Profits Easy LLC

Profitsdaily123@aol.com

facebook.com/MakeProfitsEasy

Table of Contents

Introduction

"Full many a wonder is told us in stories old, of heroes worthy of praise, of hardships dire, of joy and feasting, of weeping and of wailing; of the fighting of bold warriors; now ye may hear wonders told." (From *Nibelungenlied;* Anonymous poet circa 1180-1210)

VIKINGS! Just hearing the name conjures images of big bold men with plaited beards in horned helmets and women in armored breastplates, fighting as one, plundering villages, defending their homeland or traveling across raging seas in dragon boats seeking adventure and wealth. But there's a lot more to the legends of the Vikings than one might suspect.

In this book, you'll get a wonderful glimpse into what life must have been like for this democratic society of heathen Scandinavians: how they lived, worshipped, warred, created and expanded; where they made their homes, what they valued and why. And finally, how the Age of the Vikings came to an end.

From their ingeniously designed ships to their volatile gods and goddesses of Valhalla, from Eirik Blood-Axe to Thorfinn Skull-Splitter, the feared seamen and plunderers of the Viking Age ruled Norway, Sweden, and Denmark, then Iceland, England, Normandy, and Ireland, and roamed as far as Byzantium, Greenland, France, Russia, Spain, and North America. They were raiders, but they were also traders, settlers, craftsmen, and ingenious builders and navigators of the sea.

The history of the Vikings never seems to lose its capacity to captivate us today in much the same way as the original Viking warriors struck fear in the unsettled world of their own time. From the first documented raid to the Vikings' last stand, this is not a dry history, but a thought-provoking and often electrifying look at the lives, deaths and events that made the Vikings the formidable culture they were.

Editor's Note: All text in *italics* is directly quoted from translations of ancient literature. Text in "quotations" are a summary of portions of stories from ancient poetic literature. Text in [brackets] has been added to quotes and translations by the author for clarification.

Chapter 1: The Age of the Vikings: AD 790 to 1115

"He who lives without discipline dies without honor." Icelandic Proverb

So who were the Vikings and how did they become what they were and what they continue to be in our memories? What made these people stand out from all the rest of the warring peoples around the globe?

A lot of the Viking legend and its place in history has been misinterpreted because what we know about them comes from Skaldic and Eddic poetry, known as *sagas*, written as long as 300 years after the end of the Viking Age, and in many cases, by family members who may have embellished the feats of their ancestors. From those translations of the old writings, and from original Viking runes and other archeological findings, historians have been able to piece together a comprehensive picture of the world of the medieval Scandinavians known as the Viking

Norsemen, but it has often been difficult to discern fact from fable.

Poetic sagas may be prejudiced because they are intimately bound up with family and genealogical background. For example, in *Islendingabok* (The Book of the Icelanders), the author exaggerates the importance of the deeds of family members, and in *Heimskringla* (The Lives of the Norse Kings), claims to political power and the significance of the author's own ancestors cannot be taken as completely accurate. Like all history, however, its fluidity is developed as historians and archeologists unearth new material or create different perspectives.

So the construction of history written by authors who wanted to flatter their ancestors, along with the popular modern media of television and film, and even 19th century writings such as the *Lord of the Rings* has compromised history to some extent, but the original *Sagas* offer the best account of events and their causes taken in context.

Additionally, sophisticated techniques such as numismatic analysis, dendrochronology, which permits highly accurate dating of wooden objects by tree-ring analysis, archeo-zoology, paleo-botany, DNA analysis, ice crystallography, and climate analysis have given us considerable information to make up for any loss in translation and literary conversion.

Who Were the Vikings?

"Hail, All Father, wise warrior, one-eyed wanderer. Come sit at my fire and tell me your wisdom stories. You who chooses the slain, when my time comes to run the sky with you, let my end be worthy of song."

The Viking Age is an often misunderstood and complicated period in history, and it has been written about mostly in broad strokes, but the popular image of these independent people is often seen as one of marauding warriors who pirated the seas and plundered villages and holy places, burning everything and taking the spoils and resources for themselves. They did indeed pillage their way along the shores of Northern Europe and beyond, but Norse society at home was one of the first democratic states, and as you will see, the Vikings were not only ingenious builders, they had a great deal to do with the development of Britain and the expansion of Christianity beyond the British Isles.

Before we get into how they became known as the Norsemen, the legend we've come to know, it will be helpful to understand something about Viking names to lessen any confusion. In those days, men were named for their fathers. The names are patronymic, they're not family names as we know them where the same surname is carried on to each generation, both male and female.

A man would be addressed by his first name. For example, Leif Eriksson was called Leif, and any attribution was added to that name

- Leif the Lucky. His surname would be his father's first name. Leif was the son of Eirik Thorvaldsson, so Leif Eriksson was "Leif, Eirik's son".

Eirik Thorvaldsson (Eirik the Red) was the son of Thorvald Aswaldsson, the son of Asvald Ulfsson, the son of Ulf Oxen-Thorisson, the son of Oxen-Thorir, and so on. Here is where they begin having only one name. So you can see how each successive generation took the name of the one before.

Oxen-Thorir > Ulf Oxen-Thorirsson > Asvald Ulfsson > Thorvald Asvaldsson > Eirik Thorvaldsson > Leif Eriksson.

Oxen-Thorir: This name would have been written as *Þórir* and was a given male name. The word "oxen" before his given name would have to do with his occupation, pastime, an outstanding physical quality, or a particular temperament for which he might have been known. Oxen-Thorir was the brother of Naddodd, the discoverer of Snaeland

(Snowland/Iceland), and this is where the story of the men who would eventually become known as Vikings begins.

The Beginning of the Viking Age

"Better it is to die in battle with honor than to live in shame because you did not defend your people." Bjarnar Saga, *Hítdælakappa*

The Viking Age began with raids by these heathen Scandinavians on Christian targets in the British Isles in 793 and is contained within the Germanic Iron Age, sometimes called the Merovingian Period after the Frankish Merovingian dynasty that was the dominant power in Europe from about 460 to 751. The term "Viking Age" within the Iron Age was created by historians for the large number of seafaring raids by Scandinavian warriors that had taken place over more than 300 years and were recognized for their importance in cultural history.

One of the most often told accounts in history, and one which paints a picture for us of the mindset of these people, has to do with the feud between Eirik Thorvaldsson and his neighbor, a man called Thorgest, and it sets the scene for the development and expansion of these sea-faring people.

In pre-Christian, North-Germanic clan culture in Scandinavia, people were obligated to take revenge for the deaths or injury of their loved ones by others, regardless of the reason. In order to settle disputes so that feudal wars between clans could be avoided, a very civilized assembly called an *althing*, sort of a court hearing, took place at a designated place and time to hear all sides of an argument. In the old language, the word could be translated as "law thing", "general thing of the people" or "great thing", but all Icelandic translations contain the word for "thing".

The *althing* took place at regular intervals and was responsible for electing kings and chieftains. Among other responsibilities, they legislated law and judged disputes accordingly. Each local assembly had a law speaker or judge who presided over the hearings, with the assembly consisting of the heads of clans and free men. The rule of law was one man - one vote.

Thorvald Ásvaldsson was born in Norway and was later exiled during the reign of King Harald Fairhair for the crime of manslaughter, at which time he travelled to Snowland (Iceland) with his son, Eirik, who eventually owned his own farm. He married and soon after, his father's fate befell him, too.

It's unclear which of the stories are true. Some say a neighbor, Thorgest, borrowed a shovel, others say he borrowed some timber, and still others say it was the seat logs for a boat. When the items were not returned, Eirik took them back and the dispute ended in the death of Thorgest.

In a second crime, some of Eirik's thralls (slaves) accidentally caused a landslide on the farm of a man named Valthjof, who in turn killed the slaves. Once again, Eirik sought revenge and killed Valthjof.

The *Saga of Eirik the Red* (Eirik's Saga) recounts the story in this way:

"Then did Eirik's thralls cause a landslip on the estate of Valthjof, at Valthjofsstadr. Eyjolf the Foul, his kinsman, slew the thralls beside Skeidsbrekkur above Vatzhorn. In return Eirik slew Eyjolf the Foul; he slew also Hrafn the Dueller at Leikskalar. Gerstein and Odd of Jorfi, kinsman of Eyjolf, were found willing to follow up his death by a legal prosecution; and then was Eirik banished from Haukadalr."

A clear and likely translation from the *Saga* goes like this:

Eirik then moved to the island of Öxney (Iceland). He asked Thorgest (Þórgestr) to keep his *setstokkr* which his father had brought from

Norway. When he had finished his new house, he went back to get them, but they "could not be obtained". Erik then went to Breidabolstad and took them.

"Stein the Much-Sailing...dwelt at Breidabolstead. His son was Thorgest. Thorvald, the son of Asvald, the son of Ulf, the son of Oxe-Thorir, and Eirek the Red, his son went, for the sake of manslaughters, and settled on the Hornstrands. Eirek then went from the north and cleared land in Haukadalr [Hawksdale]. *There the thralls of Eirik let fall a rock-slip upon the dwelling of Valthjof, but his kinsman slew the thralls and Eiriks's kinsmen slew the kinsmen of Valthjof, whose kinsmen took up the blood-suit. Then was Eirik exiled.*

"...he then settled at Oxey...and left seat-beams with Thorgest; afterwards Eirek claimed his seat-beams and could not obtain them; he took the seat-beams from Breidabolstead, and Thorgest went after him; they fought and there fell two sons of Thorgest and some other men;

thereupon both sides sat at home amidst an armed company."

The seat beams that Eirek took were likely Thorgest's *setstokkr*, although the sagas are somewhat unclear. However, it makes sense that if they were indeed Eirik's seat beams, Thorgest might not have been angry enough to pursue him into a battle to the death.

"After that they both kept a large body of men together. Styr gave assistance to Eirik, as also did Eyjolf, of Sviney, Thorbjorn Vifilsson, and the sons of Thorbrand of Alptafjordr [Swanfirth]. *But the sons of Thord Gellir, as also Thorgeir of Hitardalr* [Hotdale], *Aslak of Langadalr* [Longdale], *and Illugi, his son, gave assistance to Thorgest."*

Setstokker are inherited ornamented beams believed to be of significant mystical value. They are planking beams used between the platform that ran along the sidewalls and the unfloored center of a great hall. The platform was used as a sitting and/or sleeping place by household members, and in ancient dwellings, *setstokker* were believed to hold the spirit of the elder wise householders and the wisdom of the ancestors who slept or sat on them.

So it's easy to understand why Eirik wanted these items back and why he was so furious when Thorgest refused to return them.

The outcome of the decision regarding Eirik the Red was that he was banished from the mainland of Iceland for three years. This event led him and a group of followers to travel to the lands nearly 500 miles west of Iceland.

But the question of why raiding on northern Britain began in 793 remains. Why not 50 years earlier or later?

Their homeland consisted of Iceland (Snowland, Snaeland) Denmark (Danevirke), southern Sweden, Norway (The North Way), and Jutland (northern Germany). To the south was the Frankish territory and to the west lay what is now Britain (England, Wales, Ireland, and Scotland).

The population density in the entire Scandinavian area during the early Viking Age has been estimated at 1-2 people per square kilometer or 2/3 of a mile, so the figure does not support the theory of over population. There is no record of natural disasters which might have wiped out crops or livestock, or any plague or disease. In fact, these tribes were quite self-sufficient, living off the land, farming and fishing.

The exile of Eirik the Red from both Norway and Iceland forced him to roam the sea to other lands with his men, and fighting was certainly necessary to defend their ships and property. Dynasties were growing stronger and with that came a more centralized power which likely led to conflict among the tribes. Those contenders who were unsuccessful may have decided to try their luck elsewhere. But none of these circumstances would account for the rage and barbarianism for which the Viking warriors were renowned, so historians have looked outside local circumstances for the answer.

The three major political powers in the world at that time were the Byzantine Empire in the east, the Franks to the south, and the Muslims south of the Frankish Empire.

The Byzantine Empire had survived the break-up of the Roman Empire and was remote from the Scandinavian lands. It would be more or less able to dictate the terms of its encounters with the Viking phenomenon. The Muslims had expanded during the years 660 to 830 as far east as Turkistan and Asia Minor, in Kazakhstan, north of what is now Afghanistan. This expansion pushed trade routes northward and created ideal conditions for piracy in the North Sea.

The Roman Empire had disappeared in the west due to the Frankish invasion and the Franks established themselves as the dominant tribe in what is now northern France, Belgium and western Germany. They would prove to be the most profoundly involved with the Vikings.

When Charles became the Frankish ruler in 771, his sole mission was to expand Christianity, and this is what characterized his reign and earned him the appellation of Charlemagne, Charles the Great. He stopped the Muslim expansion, drove back the Arabs, established dominance in Spain and Gaul, removed the Lombards from power in Italy, pushed back the Slavs, and reached his authority – and that of the Christian Church – as far north as the lower Scandinavian peninsula.

Here he crossed the rivers and destroyed the Irmensul, the sacred wooden pillar that was the Saxons' holy shrine, and this, it's believed, was the turning point which cohered the heathens into turning against the Christians. This was the single deciding event that was the direct trigger for the distinctive period known as the Viking Age.

"While the king spent the winter at the villa of Quierzy, he decided to attack the treacherous tribe of the Saxons until they were defeated, forced to accept the Christian religion, or entirely exterminated."

He persisted with baptisms and threats of death, invasion of lands and exile for any who did not accept Christianity. He destroyed religious sanctuaries and the cultural institutions of those who refused his terms, so the Saxons returned in kind. They attacked and burned Christian churches and monasteries.

Most of the information we have about Viking raids comes from Christian sources which talk about the massacres and atrocities of monks and nuns, but very little about what had been previously inflicted on the pagans by the armies of Charlemagne. It's easy to understand that the violence inflicted on Christian establishments had its origin in a dramatic cultural and religious conflict.

The local Scandinavian cultures that felt the first shock of the threat of Charlemagne were not compacted in one localized group. They were not organized into any kind of structure and too small in number to mount any kind of military defense against Frankish Christendom, so they looked for a soft target, what we might call an easy mark, and the undefended monastery at Lindisfarne, the first successful raid, fit the bill.

Chapter 2: Raiders from the North: The Norsemen

Let me feel fury and joy, and understand sacrifice. Let me think long, remember well and journey far. Odin, witness this."

The word "Viking" is believed to have come from the Scandinavian word *vik*, which means bay or creek, and Vik, the name for the bay area of south eastern Norway around Oslo. This was the root of the word *vikingr* or pirate, and literature suggests that the Vik Fjord was the most heavily trafficked maritime area in the region at the time.

The Old Norse verb *víkja* means "to travel from place to place". Other descriptions use the word *saewicingas*, which means "sea warriors' (from the old English poem *Exodus*). The poetic skalds (poets) refer to "long-distance sea warriors" in a positive context, and the *Poetic Edda*, a collection of poems from a later period, uses the same reference. Rune stones from

Sweden and Denmark talk about *fara í viking*, "to go on a viking expedition" and men were said to be "going viking", indicating that they were going pirating. However, in some parts of modern-day England settled by Scandinavians, the word *viking* denotes "vandal, barbarian, thug, hooligan, violent, and dangerous people".

Originally, the Vikings were not a unified group or tribe of men. They were simply a conglomerate of chieftain-led tribes from Denmark, Norway and Sweden that generally fought against each other, and of course, they didn't call themselves Vikings. They had no military coherency and lived according to the laws of the *althing,* the general council of leaders and elders.

They left their homelands for several reasons, including the search for riches, but cultural relativity makes it somewhat difficult to view them as they really were. We tend to describe them as raiders, traders, travelers, explorers, and shipbuilding geniuses, and they were all those things, but they were far from being a group of adolescent young men who stepped on shore and roughed up the locals a bit. They were indeed a brutal force of violence against the onslaught of Christianity and showed no regard for anything or anyone who may have had the misfortune to be in their path.

"They caused the bloody eagle to be carved on the back of Ælla, and they cut away all the ribs from the spine and ripped out his lungs...and that was [also] *Halfdan's death."*

They set out in what seemed to be a rage of indifference for the humanity of their Christian victims equal to that of Charlemagne's on the Saxons, deliberately drowning monks as if to demonstrate some travesty of baptism, and blaspheming holy altars and treasures in the same way the Franks had destroyed the Irmensul.

"They cut up Bible clasps and crosses and reshaped them into items of personal

ornamentation" in what was apparently an overt display of cultural disrespect.

And so it was that the pagans or heathens, who were referred to in terms of their religion, became *flotman, saeman, sceigdman,* or *aescman* – all terms for seaborne raiders, and would eventually be known as Vikings.

Iceland

Iceland is described in the *Historia Norwegie* as having "*innumerable mountains overlaid with unmelting glaciers, whose whole surface twitches like Etna, and when it is shaken with a horrifying earth tremor, it belches up sulfurous fireballs.*"

There are several accounts in the *Landnámabók* (*Book of the Settlements*) of who might have been the first to set foot on what is now Iceland. Many historians think Irish monks had settled the island in the 8th century, and fled when the Norwegians came.

In the 9th century, a Norwegian named Nadodd, who had set out for the Faroe Islands, found himself going ashore near what is now Reydarfjord, and finding no inhabitants, called the place Snaeland (Snowland). Another discovery was made by a Swede named Gardar Svavarsson who got lost on his way to the Hebrides, and he called the place Gardarholm or Gardar's Island. But neither stayed long enough to settle the island.

The first attempt to settle Iceland came from Floki Vilgerdasson and a small group who *"found the waters so well stocked with fish and seals that they neglected to make hay for their livestock for the winter"*, and so the animals died. Vilgerdasson named the place Iceland and planned to settle there, but the bitter cold proved too much for his group and they went back to Norway.

In Ari Thorgilsson's *Book of the Icelanders*, Ingólfur Arnarsson traveled from Norway to Iceland for the first time "*when*

Harald Finehair [Harald Fairhair] *was sixteen years old*", circa 874, and most authorities consider his group to be the first settlers. He was a chieftain who built his farm in Reykjavík, the site of the present capital.

More settlers came over a 60 year period from Scandinavia and Ireland, and by 930, the land was completely settled and a government was established.

Back in Norway, Thorvald Ásvaldsson was being exiled by Harald Fairhair for the crime of manslaughter, so he and his son Eirik traveled to Iceland. When Eirik got into his dispute with his neighbor Thorgest and Thorgest was killed, Eirik Thorvaldsson spent his 3 years in exile from Iceland traveling to the lands 500 miles west, to what is now Greenland.

Greenland

Apparently no one was exempt from the laws and sentences of the courts, and according to the *Book of the Icelanders*, "*many chieftains were convicted or exiled for manslaughter or assault*", and somewhere around the year 980, such was the case for Erik the Red-Beard, leader of the Viking Age colonists who settled Greenland.

The law as stated in the *Grágás* said that for the most severe crime, a man might be declared a *skógarmaðr* (a man of the forest), and that he must live apart in the forests or other deserted places. He was relieved of his property and goods, and no one was allowed to shelter him. It was a crime to help him leave the country. Should he manage to do so, he was forbidden to return. Anyone had permission to kill him without the consequence of lawful retribution.

For a lesser crime, *heraðssekt* was passed, which meant a man must be exiled to a particular district for a designated period of time and he was forbidden to use the main road more often than once a month. Eirik's sentence fell between the two. He must pay a fine, leave

Iceland within three summers and remain away for another three.

But apparently, Eirik had other plans for his life and was not about to hang around in idol isolation for three years.

From the *Book of the Settlement of Iceland*:

"*Eirek and his party were outlawed at the Thorsness Thing. Then he fitted out a ship in Eireksvag, but Eyjolf hid him in Dimunvag while Thorgest's party were seeking him about the islands. Thorbjorn and Eyjolf and Styr followed Eirek out beyond the islands; he told them that he purposed to seek that land which Gunnbjorn, the son of Ulf Crow, saw when being driven west, beyond Iceland, by a storm; he found there Gunnbjorn's skerries... [And] if he discovered land he would afterwards revisit his friends.*"

When he finally left, he followed the route of Gunnbjørn Ulfsson who had sighted unknown land in the southwest. These are believed to have been the islands off the east coast of Greenland.

"But the third summer he went north as far as Snæfell...and was the third winter in Eirek's Island. Later in the summer, Eirek went to settle that land which he had found, and which he called Greenland, for he said that many men would desire to visit if he gave the land a good name."

Three years later, he returned to Iceland and solicited 10 chieftains to accompany him to the new land, and they set sail with a fleet of 25 ships, only 14 having made it to their destination.

"So the men of lore say that that summer twenty-five ships went to Greenland from Broadfirth and Borgfirth, and that fourteen got through to the west, that certain of them were driven back and some were lost...fifteen years before Christian faith was made law in Iceland."

The land was settled in two distinct areas: what are known as the Eastern and Western Settlements, though both were actually located in the south. The Eastern settlement was located on the southwestern tip of Greenland along the coast that stretches in a fjord-lined ribbon between the glaciers and the sea, about 200 miles east of the Western Settlement because of the geography of the coastline. The Western settlement was located about 400 miles north, also on the western coast.

Daily life consisted of much the same that they were accustomed to in Iceland and Norway: tending small fields, farming cows, horses, pigs, and goats, with sheep kept for their wool and milk. Bear, reindeer, hares, and birds were hunted and trapped; whales, walrus and seals were hunted at sea, and the fjords were fished for cod and salmon.

Wool was spun for blankets and clothing.

In 1990, a group of archeologists from Greenland University and the Danish National

Museum uncovered a farm east of Nuuk, under the permafrost, about 60 miles from the coast at the heart of what would have been the Western Settlement. It's estimated that this farm was occupied for 300 years, from the 11th to the 14th centuries. Based on the items that were left behind, researchers believe the inhabitants left in a hurry.

Stone and turf were used to build the main house and wood was used for the interior with benches that ran along the walls on both sides of the main room.

A cooking pit was found, a fireplace, an oven, a stable for animals, textile fragments, spindle whorls and warp weights, part of an upright loom, and as many as 63 rooms had been added to the main house estimated to have been built over 8 distinct phases of building activity. Roofing was a patchwork of branches, turfs and loose joists held up by wooden posts on flat stones.

Household items made from soapstone, horn, reindeer antler, bone, and wood were found, along with dice and gaming pieces, and tiny scaled-down versions of vessels, possibly made for children. The names Thor and Bardr and Björk were carved in runes on the lid of a wooden box along with a dragon's head and vines.

The disappearance of the inhabitants of the Western Settlement remains a mystery, though it was likely due to the sheer difficulty of living in the harsh environment, a fate which ended the larger Eastern Settlement a century later. Climatologists believe that the end of the Medieval Warm Period and the beginning of what's known as the Little Ice Age had much to do with pushing the Vikings into the adventures that led to trade with the Arabs of the Iberian Peninsula and the tribes of the Volga.

The *Konungs Skuggská* (*King's Mirror*) written in 1250 tells us:

"Everything that comes from other lands is high in price, for this land lies so distant from other countries that men seldom visit it. And everything that is needed to improve the land must be purchased abroad, both iron and all the timber used in building houses."

Although the climate may have contributed to the expansion and exploration of the Norsemen, as we've seen, the biggest catalyst was something far more compelling for these loyal clansmen: the destruction of their most holy relic by armies of the Catholic Church and the killing of innocents who would not convert to Christianity.

Chapter 3: Viking Warfare and Tactics

"Lo, there do I see my father; Lo, there do I see my mother and my brothers and my sisters. Lo, there do I see the line of my people back to the beginning. Lo, they do call to me; they bid me take my place among them in the halls of Valhalla where thine enemies have been vanquished; where the brave shall live forever. Nor shall we mourn, but rejoice for those that have died the glorious death."

Once raiding started and strategies began to develop, the squadrons known collectively as the Vikings became more cunning and clever in their attempts to outwit and out-maneuver the large armies of the enemy.

Creating Psychological Terror

Warriors did whatever they could to give themselves an advantage in battle, including making themselves appear bigger, mightier and more fearsome, filing their teeth to look more like those of animals, with a distinctive horizontal groove halfway up, and painting their eyes and skin, something akin to "war paint" or modern tattoos.

"From the tips of his toes to his neck, each man is tattooed dark green with designs, with eye markings that made him appear exotic, disconcerting or alarming, and they contorted their faces into grotesque and frightening masks. They display no empathy for their victims and show extreme violence and savagery on the battlefield."

Some Viking warriors were known as *berserkers*, an Old Norse term used for those special few who, according to the *Sagas*, "fought naked or scantily clad, deliberately inducing themselves into a battle frenzy which seemed to transform them into extraordinary beings beyond the ken of most, having superhuman strength which allowed them to feel no pain in their delirium."

At some point, warfare for the Vikings may have come to the point of being an elitist activity, with a focus on personal gain rather than religious revenge, but part of the value system of Viking war is almost unrestricted legion, and a man would suffer unimaginable blows in defense of his fellows, his honor and his memory so that he might enter Valhalla. Here's a brutal example of the type of atrocity these men inflicted and withstood in battle:

An excavation in England unearthed the body of a man aged 35-45, buried with a sword, a small Thor's hammer and a boar's tusk. The bones show that the warrior died a savage and brutal death. Two wounds on his skull were probably made by a spear and marks on the spine suggest the warrior was disemboweled after death.

The man was also stabbed in the head, jaw, arm and thigh. Each of his toes and both his heels were split lengthways. A violent blow to the top of the thigh could have removed his genitals, and it's believed this was the reason for placing the boar's tusk between his legs. The Vikings believed that a body could not enter Valhalla if it was not whole, so this may have been an attempt by those who buried him to make his body whole before his journey to the afterlife.

Longphorts

The Vikings started out as part-time raiders, "going viking" in early spring and returning home in autumn, but over time and as battles became more important as territorial conquests and bids for thrones rather than as mere religious revenge, they often stayed where they were rather than returning to their farms and settlements. They began to overwinter on the outlying islands of Ireland in the late 830s, and by 837, as many as 60 ships at a time could be seen camping and raiding along the inland lakes.

"The plundering of Lughmhadh by the foreigners made prisoners of many bishops and

other wise and learned men, and carried them to their fortress."

The fortress referred to in this text is the *longphort*, sometimes referred to as a ringfort. It was a ship camp created to protect vessels and men over the cold months, and in this way, the Viking fleets were able to reserve resources and stay close to the territories they were trying to obtain.

Originally, longphorts were simply a D-shaped earthen bank and ditch put up on the landward side of a beached ship so the vessel could easily be defended. They were set along shorelines, at tributaries or rivers, and ultimately grew into settlements that provided stopping points along trade routes, establishing Viking presence in Ireland in places such as Dublin, Cork, Waterford, Wexford, and Limerick.

These were no longer small enclosures, and were often built to encompass several ships measuring 80 feet or more each, with the depth of the ground which the enclosure surrounded being almost equal to the length. They could have been as high as 8-10 feet or more with constructed dwellings built into the earthen wall.

Longphorts have been variously described by historians and archeologists as a defended ship harbor, an emporium or trading station and a shore fortress. The *Royal Irish Academy Dictionary* defines a longphort as "a camp, encampment, temporary stronghold, fortress, mansion or princely dwelling."

So the longphort evolved from being a simple barricade to keep out invaders and protect ships to the Viking settlements themselves and then to large trading cities. Ath Cliath, a Viking longphort that became the city of Dublin, is believed to have been built around 840. Archeologists have unearthed post holes, refuse pits, ship rivets, and grave goods, suggesting that Ath Cliath was used to transport silver, slaves, and other market goods in trade.

Fire

The Vikings had a very unique technique for carrying fire with them. They collected a fungus from a certain tree bark and boiled it for several days in urine. They then pounded the substance until it was dense and flat, something like felt. The sodium nitrate in the urine would allow the material to smolder without burning until such time as they wanted a flame, then they would fan the spark. In this way, they could have fire rather quickly anywhere they went.

Coastal Blockades

Another Viking tactic used to prevent approaching enemy squadrons from getting too close to their shores and trading stations or entering their harbors was the coastal blockade, borrowed from the early Iron Age, in which ships would be deliberately sunk in several strategic places. Some blockades consisted of underwater piles of timbers or stones that were strewn in shallow water, and all this was complemented by lookout stations on coastal hills from which signals could be relayed using beacon fires (yes, just like in the movies).

Think of the manpower and time it would have taken to cut, drag and sink timber, build lookouts by carrying timber up high hills, erect earthen banks, dig ditches, and supply needs for the winter. The Viking sense of teamwork was one of their greatest assets.

Of course, it's well known that the design and construction of the Viking ships was their greatest accomplishment in terms of war, trade and exploration, and these ships are described in detail in Chapter 5: *Viking Ingenuity: The Shipbuilders*. They were light and fast, and could be easily maneuvered onto the beach in places that no traditional ship could go, and to this they owe a good portion of their success in raiding.

Flyting

Another tactic of the Vikings was to play a game of do or dare, something referred to as a *flyting* match, in which they would give their victims the opportunity to buy them off rather than suffer the invasion. It was a form of blackmailing piracy at its best. One story told in the Old English poem, *The Battle of Maldon*, describes a real battle between the English army commanded by Byrhtnoth of Essex and a mixed band of Vikings led by Olaf Tryggvason.

"On the beach there stood, calling out sternly, a Viking messenger who boastfully spoke the sea rovers' demands to the earl, standing there on the shore. 'It would be better for you to buy off quickly this rush of spears with tax than that we, rough fighter as we are, should engage in battle. What need for us to kill each other if you will just agree?'

"But Byrhtnoth would not consent and thus spake, 'Our riches will not come to you so easily. Spear point and sword's edge shall decide between us, grim war-play indeed, before we give tribute'." In this battle, Byrhtnoth is killed.

Armor and Weapons

The Vikings were much feared all along the coast of Europe because their incursions into the land meant that they could burn and pillage to their heart's content. There were no armies in small villages or in the remote areas where most monasteries were located. There was no defense to speak of, at least in the beginning.

They had the unrivaled mobility of their longships, which at first were typically deployed in squadrons of 3-5 ships, but by the 9th century, they moved in groups of 30 ships. By the year 875, Viking fleets often consisted of more than one hundred invading ships. These ships could carry substantial quantities of supplies which were replenished from their plundering, and warriors were thus able to be sustained for years at a time away from home.

Basic spears, bows and arrows were cheap to make because they used very little iron, and they could be used for other things such as hunting. Axes doubled as domestic tools. But swords needed to be exceptional and even a basic sword needed a lot of iron or steel as well as the technical skill to forge it.

An analysis of archeological finds shows that the later Vikings were using steel known to have come from the Islamic world, and the hilts were often highly decorated and distinctively shaped. Carolingian hilts (Frankish empire) have been found throughout the Viking world from Ireland to the Ukraine. But only the rich could afford swords, so it's likely that the Vikings also had mail shirts and helmets, also costly items, that rivaled those of the Frankish armies and which contributed to their success on the battlefield. In fact, because the Vikings did not make their own weapons, Frankish laws of the early 9th century forbade the provision of horses or weapons to the Vikings.

Sword chapes, the protective fitting on the lower end of a sword scabbard, were also used. Although this was not weaponry, it signaled the self-styled importance of the identity of the warrior because it was always on display, unlike the sword blade itself.

Though they may have existed, there is no real evidence to support the romantic image of Viking helmets adorned with horns or wings except for those worn by gods in later paintings. Instead, they were more like Roman cavalry helmets, basically bullet shaped and highly ornamented with intricately detailed designs in the metal, and with nose, cheek and neck guards. Mail neck guards replaced solid metal guards around the 10th century.

Chapter 4: Viking Expansion: The Raiders

Once the raids began, Viking warriors came from the sea with a thirst for vengeance, terrorizing in a remarkable fashion that lasted 300 years and which left the world with an enduring legacy.

The First Raid

The first major raid of note on Lindisfarne in 793 was made off the coast of what is now north eastern England, but there were some earlier attacks by pagan seamen along the English Channel coast in 792. These were reported as disturbances.

Monasteries were known to house elaborate wealth in the form of reliquaries, chalices, pyxes (holy boxes which held the Eucharist), crosses, and crosiers which decorated the sanctuary, and because the monasteries were generally unprotected and in remote areas, they were particularly easy targets. The success of this raid led to other raids on holy places and religious centers.

Lindisfarne was particularly wealthy, so much so that several Viking raids still had not depleted its coffers. The carved oak reliquary coffin of Saint Cuthbert remained untouched and when it was opened in 1827, it still contained the treasures that had been buried with the saint. The Vikings either missed the silver encased portable altar that was directly adjacent or they had some fear of defiling it which had to do with consequences that might affect their own afterlife.

Recreations of the event have shown that in good weather, when visibility was high, ships could be seen from the monastery up to 18 nautical miles away. This distance could be covered in about one hour. Since this was the first raid, the residents of the monastery viewed the ships as friendly. In subsequent raids, one hour was all the time they had to prepare for a defense, limited as that might be. And because the Vikings were skilled at sailing without benefit of the sun, with no worries about running the ships aground, they could stage their raids in any weather, leaving their victims no time at all to hide their treasures and themselves.

According to reports at the time in the *Anglo-Saxon Chronicle*, the weather condition during the raid on Lindesfarne was one of "high winds and lightning flashes" which would be interpreted today as stormy and with poor visibility. In this way, the Vikings were able to gain closer access without being seen.

Simeon Durham wrote in the 12th century:

"And they came to the church at Lindisfarne, laid everything waste with grievous plundering, trampled the holy places with polluted steps, dug up the altars and seized all the treasure of the holy church. They killed some of the brothers, took some away with them in fetters, many they drove out, naked and loaded with insults, some they drowned in the sea..."

Picture stones have given us information beyond runes and letters that graphically depict events, and these large stones have been found throughout England and Scandinavia. The Lindisfarne stone shows an image that is strikingly similar to one which appears on a panel of the Gotland Hammars picture stone of Stora Hammars parish in Gotland, Sweden - seven marching men in profile, five carrying axes and two carrying swords. The men wear tunics that reach to mid-thigh and have padding around the midriff, with heavy ankle-high shoes and axes raised high as if prepared to sweep.

England

The larger religious centers owned land and money generally acquired by donations to the church, but they also held the treasures of the sanctuary which could be easily carried back to the Vikings' ships. In this letter written in the wake of the attack on St. Cuthbert's Church, a wealthy Christian center, Alcuin, one of the leading Christian figures of the time, addresses King Ethelred of Northumbria:

"We and our fathers have now lived in this fair land for nearly three hundred and fifty years, and never before has such an atrocity been seen in Britain. The church of St. Cuthbert is spattered with the blood of the priests of God, stripped of all its furnishings, exposed to the plundering of pagans, a place more sacred than any in Britain."

He talks about the "pagan war band that arrived from the ends of the earth" and berates the king for copying the ways of the pagans who "cut their hair and beards."

In another account, a 12th century English chronicler writes:

"In the same year, the pagans from the northern regions came with a naval force to Britain like stinging hornets and spread on all sides like fearful wolves, robbed, tore and slaughtered not only beasts of burden, sheep

and oxen, but even priests and deacons, and companies of monks and nuns."

Across northern Europe, coastal communities were now becoming vigilant, shoring up their resources and anticipating attacks. Charlemagne set up post forts and ships at main ports, ready to deploy to areas of Viking strikes which were now occurring in England, France, Spain, the Mediterranean islands, the North African coast, the Rhone valley, and as far as Italy.

In another raid, the Vikings plundered Ecgfrith's monastery at Donemuthan in Northumbria. Simeon of Durham wrote:

"You live by the sea from whence this plague first came, yet the great protector at St. Cuthbert's has not allowed the heathens to go away unpunished, for their chief was killed by the English with a cruel death, and after a short space of time, the violence of a storm battered, destroyed and broke to pieces their ships, and the sea overwhelmed many of them. Some were

cast on the shore and soon killed without mercy. And these things befell them rightly, for they had gravely injured those who had not injured them."

In this passage, we see that the Vikings, who were seemingly invulnerable, were only too human. The storm which overtook their ships must have been extremely violent, and when some were washed ashore, they must have been exhausted because they were easily overcome by the English who "killed them without mercy".

Ireland

At first, the forays into Ireland were confined to the coast, but by the 830s, the Vikings had begun to penetrate the inland rivers, plundering the great monasteries one by one. A writing found in the margin of a book by an unknown monk in an isolated monastery in southwest Ireland reads:

"*Fierce and wild is the wind tonight. It tosses the tresses of the sea to white. On such a night, I may take my ease, for the fierce Northmen only course the quiet seas.*"

Ireland had become a target. The Vikings had discovered the custom of housing the remains of the Christian's revered dead in sumptuous containers of gold and silver, so the potential of these territories in funding Viking activities was vast. As the threat grew, the 150 kings of Ireland began to battle against the heathens, joined by a militarized church leadership, putting abbots into the field at the head of their own monastic armies, and in 811, there was a "slaughtering of the pagans."

More monasteries and churches than are enumerable were plundered, some 2 and 3 times over in coastal areas, but this was a prelude to larger and more organized raiding that led to the possibility of settlements and colonization.

Raids throughout Iceland and Greenland were rampant. Other raids included Scotland in 795, when the undefended monasteries of Skye and Iona were attacked. The outlying islands of the Hebrides off the west coast of Scotland were easy targets for Viking strikes.

"The devastation of all the islands of Britain by the heathens; the Isle of Skye was overwhelmed and laid waste; Iona, more sacred than any, was burned down and the community of people killed."

On the island of Inchmarnock in southwest Scotland, an inscribed stone was found depicting three Vikings in chain mail armor dragging a monk in fetterlock (handcuffs) to their ship.

A report in the *Royal Frankish Annals* for the year 809 talks about an attack of an envoy at sea and the kidnapping of a deacon who was held for ransom, and though the report only refers to "pirates", the attack had all the earmarks of a Viking enterprise. From 835 onward, a Viking raid took place every year, and battles between the English and the pirates were reported in the *Anglo-Saxon Chronicle.*

Great slaughters took place in London, Sheppey, along the Thames, Portland, and Rochester, but thus far, raiding was only seasonal. Viking fleets would arrive in the spring, raid throughout the summer and early autumn, and then hole up for the winter. But in the winter of 851, according to the *Chronicle*, 350 ships entered the Thames and attacked London and Canterbury. For the first time, they spent the winter in England, and Viking forces were moving across the country in Sheppey, the Somme River, and Winchester. This wolfish escalation of establishing winter camps foreshadowed things to come.

For a time in the years after Lindisfarne, the Vikings turned their efforts toward the Frankish empire, but the British Isles, though not as wealthy would soon come back to their attention. Ireland was filled with monasteries, still untouched by looters, and they proved a tempting target. It also had gold, silver, copper, and precious stones such as emeralds, amethysts, and topaz as well as diamonds.

Tribal warfare in Ireland had divided the island, and any attempt at unity came too late to hold off this new round of Viking invaders. Irish forces consisted of tribes, each with their own leader and acting independently. Two years after Lindesfarne, the Vikings hit, slaughtering monks, burning buildings, and carrying off livestock. The success of these Norwegian Vikings drew others, and over the next 20 years, raids became more daring and increased in some cases to 3 times a month on the same monastery. The monks fought back, but their efforts only caused the pirates to redouble their efforts, striking harder the next time.

In 836, a group of Vikings marched inland, 20 miles from the safety of the coast. In the same year, Thorgils the Devil entered the fray and set out to destroy Ireland's holiest shrine: the city of Armagh, the burial place of St. Patrick.

Thorgils and his men destroyed and defiled the holy place, killed monks and students, shattered altars, hacked tombs, and sacrificed the battle to Odin. Thorgils' goal was to conquer the entirety of Ireland. He cleverly took over the collection of duties owed to the monastery and set himself up as the new master. He is considered to be the most brutal Viking to enter Ireland, and now he needed a base of operations.

He built a longphort in a sheltered bay of the Irish Sea, a place that was conveniently located between Ireland and Britain, a place the locals named Dubh-Linn – the black pools. He built roads of timber and houses of mud and wickerwork. His goal was to build a Viking center, a Viking state with himself as king. From here, he would step up his attacks, repeating the event at Armagh in Limerick, Confert and Clonmacnoise.

Mysteriously, however, Thorgils was captured in 845 by some act of trickery by Mael

Seachlinn, a king of Tara, who had Thorgils bound, weighed down with stones and thrown into the river. The Norwegian and Danish Vikings who had been bound by a central figure were now fighting each other for control of Dublin, both sides aided by the mercenary Irish Vikings, the offspring of mixed marriages.

Olaf the White, son of the Norwegian warlord Ingjald Helgasson, led the Norwegians, and Ivar the Boneless, who arrived in force, led the Danes. The two eventually agreed to split rule of the city. Neither was interested in leading their men into the bogs and forests of the interior to take over all of Ireland. They had learned the perils of moving away from the coast.

What was more important to them now was the prosperous trade that had developed in Dublin. It had become what was probably the busiest trading port under Viking control and an important regular port of call for Vikings throughout the North Atlantic.

The Great Heathen Army of 865

The success of the Vikings raids in Ireland was due in part to the fragmented nature of the rulers in that land and their inability to mount a cohesive military defense, and the same was the case for England. These fragmented kingdoms began to emerge after the Romans withdrew in the 5th century and were always in competition with each other: Northumbria, Mercia, East Anglia, Essex, Wessex, Sussex, Kent, and parts of what is now Worcestershire, Warwickshire and Gloucestershire. By the time the Viking raids began, these smaller kingdoms had been absorbed by more powerful neighbors, yet loyalties remained tied to the smaller regions. There was no England as we know it today; no united kingdom.

The Great Heathen Army that attacked East Anglia in 865 was by far the most fearsome, in sheer numbers alone, than any raiding group that came before. Now, it seemed, the Vikings had territorial ambitions, and their goals were realized in just over 10 years.

Led by the sons of Ragnar "Hairy Breeches" Lodbrok, the 13th century *Saga of Ragnar Lodbrok and His Sons* recounts the events that led to the creation of the great army and puts the Danes in a heroic light. This unified invasion of England puts revenge for the execution of Ragnar as their motive:

"Ragnar traveled to Gotland to save a princess of that land from the enormous serpent and win the kingdom back for the people. He prepared himself with leather trousers that he boiled in pitch to prevent the venom of the monster's fangs from entering his skin. To this he added a cushion of hair beneath his clothes for padding, and as a final insurance, he leapt into the icy sea so that his breeches would freeze before meeting the serpent.

"Ragnar succeeded in his mission and moved to the land of King Aella, who threw him into a snake pit. When his tormentors realized the cause of his immunity, they removed his breeches, and his last words could be heard

carried back to his sons. 'The little pigs would grunt if they knew how the father pig has suffered.' And so it was that his sons rose to collect a great army and invade Northumberland.' "

Viking raids had previously been small-scale incursions with a "strike and get out quickly" strategy. They had focused primarily on monasteries and churches and their main goal was to plunder the wealth and treasures housed in these holy establishments. In 865, however, Viking leaders from Sweden, Norway and Denmark joined forces under a unified command and transformed their attack strategy to one of full invasion. They were no longer interested in monetary gain alone. Now they wanted to conquer England.

Led by Ivar the Boneless, a son of Ragnar, the army landed in East Anglia in 865, obtained horses and overtook Northumbria, which was experiencing a rivalry between two claimants to the throne. Contemporary annals conclude that overall, this was a well-led, organized, tactically sophisticated and highly mobile military force with very efficient lines of communication.

The Vikings now controlled Northumbria, about 25-30% of the land which is now England, and overwintered there. In 866, they marched north and captured York. For 6 more years, bloody battles ensued in the south, the heartland of Wessex, and the Heathen army seemed inexhaustible. When the Northumbrians rose to mount a counterattack, they were defeated and immense numbers were slaughtered, among them the two rival kings, Osberht and Aelle.

"Aella was killed by the attackers, the blood eagle cut into his back. He was carved with the figure of the eagle, exultant in its victory. It was Ivar, who dwelt at York, who carved the eagle in Aella's back."

The practice of "cutting the blood eagle" was a particularly gruesome form of torture, even by the standards of the day which included all sorts of axing, gouging and dismemberment.

The ribs of the victim were cut away at the spine and pulled out from behind along with the lungs. The intent was to create the image of an eagle perched on the back of the victim working its way into the flesh with its talons and beak. The victim was then dedicated to Odin.

"*... [he] made them carve an eagle on his back with a sword, and cut the ribs all from the backbone, and draw the lungs there out, and gave him to Odin for the victory he had won.*"

Ivar the Boneless was touted to be the most dreadful of all the Danish kings who ravaged the land. In another account, he is talked about like this:

"Ivar had Edmund seized and brought before him, tied him to a tree and scourged with a whip. He called on Christ, infuriating the heathens. They shot him with spears in a game until he was the image of a hedgehog, filled with bristles. They used him as a target for the archery, finally cutting off his head and throwing it into the undergrowth."

Between 867 and 870, the Vikings had installed a puppet ruler, Egbert, as king of Northumbria, taken Nottingham and Thetford, and had successfully defeated East Anglia. Only Wessex was left, and once they gained Wessex, all England would be under Viking rule.

In 871, Viking forces were once again swelled by the arrival of summer forces, but now Wessex was ruled by Alfred and the Viking forces were unable to break the West Saxon resistance. After endless numbers of battles south of the Thames occurred that year, King Alfred of Wessex and the Danes came to a peace settlement, and the Vikings returned their attention to the rest of England. Seven years later, the Vikings surprised Alfred once again.

"The Vikings army stole itself away to the West Saxons' land and settled there and drove many of the people over sea, and the rest submitted to them, except for the king, Alfred, and he, with a little band, withdrew to the

woods and moor-fastnesses, hiding in the marshes at Athelney."

Once again, the West Saxons confronted the Vikings in open battle at Edington, a turning point that found the Vikings defeated. An agreement was made and England was divided, but King Alfred was not content to let so much of England remain under Danish rule. In 866, his army took London and the Viking army turned its attention to the Franks, while other Viking raids continued along the English Channel. By 896, the Vikings were being defeated repeatedly by the armies and navy of Alfred the Great, and for about 28 years, the Anglo-Saxons and the Viking incomers under the Danelaw lived fairly peaceably in their respective territories until the Norman Conquest in 1066.

The Establishment of the Danelaw

The sixteen year period between the invasion of the Great Heathen Army and the conquest of eastern Britain would be a seminal moment in the evolution of Scandinavian history, from which many of the most colorful legends and myths about the Viking Age would be created, as well as the demographic makeup of England.

The boundaries were settled as running up the Thames, then up the Lea, along the Lea to its source, then in a straight line to Bedford, then up the Ouse to the Watling Street. This would define the regions of "all the English race and all the people which is in East Anglia." Now, the seven kingdoms, which had been reduced to four by the time of the Lindisfarne raid and to two by the time of Alfred the Great, came under the rule of one king.

The chroniclers described Alfred as "king over all England except that part which was under Danish domination, and he ruled the kingdom twenty-eight and a half years." What the chronicler left out was the fact that the Danelaw, the area under Danish rule, was very large and, by now, well established.

The new model for English monarchy was so efficient that later Scandinavian conquerors were able to take over England with little adjustment to their administration of rule.

The campaign to repossess the occupied lands was undertaken by Aethelwold, the son of Ethelred I, the last of Alfred's brothers to hold the throne of Wessex. He drove out Alfred's son, Edward, who in turn convinced the Viking Northumbrians of York to accept him as their leader. Eventually, all Viking strongholds in England fell, and the city of York's last Scandinavian ruler, the Norwegian Erik Bloodaxe, was evicted and "treacherously slain", effectively signaling the end of Scandinavian power in England.

But there was still the Viking contingent in Ireland to contend with, who were concentrated in Dublin and struggling for power among themselves. After three decades of fighting continued, the Vikings were driven out of Dublin and made for the Wirral Peninsula, where they were allowed to stay. This area of Britain was never part of the Danelaw, and this may be the reason they were allowed to thrive there.

Today there are more than 600 place names of Scandinavian origin on the Ordinance Survey maps of this area and DNA traces tell the same story. This was a large and permanent settlement for the Norwegians.

The Danelaw was not seen as something that could be decisively dismissed. The English thought that, by right of usage over time, England was inherently English. However, the concept of what the Norwegians call *hevd* – a right established not in law but in possession – is something that is relative, as proved by modern forensics.

A genetic survey carried out for the BBC by a team from University College London (UCL) headed by Professor David Goldstein in 200 found it impossible to distinguish between the

DNA of the 5th century Saxon invaders and 9th century Vikings.

"The tests looked at the Y chromosome, which is only carried by men. This chromosome is particularly useful for population-genetics studies as it is passed directly from father to son with virtually no alteration. Other chromosomes exist in pairs, one member of which is passed on from the mother and the other from the father. But because women do not carry a Y chromosome, geneticists can always be sure that this part of a man's DNA has come from his father, and from his grandfather before him. This chromosome allows geneticists to begin to unravel the male ancestry of the British Isles."

So the idea of persistent racial identity, one which lays claim to a certain territory or country, is an obstinate myth.

The Siege of Paris

The first recorded raid in continental Europe came in France in 799, at the island monastery of St Philibert's in Noirmoutier, near the Loire River on the western coast of what is now France, but the Carolingian defense, as the Vikings would soon discover, was well organized, and attacks were more or less easily beaten off. Small attacks had been going on simultaneously with those orchestrated in England and Ireland.

However the city of Paris would be the culmination of invasions throughout the kingdom, and in 845, the city was looted. The Frankish Empire was paying too much, in their view, to make the Vikings go away, yet they regularly continued to raid northern France. A monk at the monastery of Noirmoutier wrote:

"The number of ships grows and the endless stream of Vikings never ceases. Everywhere Christians are the victims of massacre, burning and plundering as they conquer all in their path and no one resists them. An innumerable fleet sailed up the Seine and the evil grows in the whole region. Rouen is laid waste, plundered and burned; Paris,

Beauvais and Meaux taken, Melun's strong fortress leveled to the ground, Chartres occupied, Evreux and Bayeux plundered and every town besieged."

A great raid of this sort, as described by the monk, is considered to have been fairly uncommon. Most of the Viking raids are thought to have consisted of no more than a hundred men, and they were uncoordinated and opportunistic. This made them harder to predict, and the uncertainty itself is what engendered fear among the communities they victimized.

In 845, however, Viking raiders came with a fleet of 120 ships, which could have held 7000 men or more, led by the legendary chieftain, Ragnar "Hairy Breeches" Lodbrok. They entered the Seine and made their way upriver to Paris where, after months of fighting the armies of King Charles the Bald, they were paid a ransom to retreat. One of the complications of making treaties with the raiders, at least as far as their enemy kings were concerned, was that there was no way to make a formal protest to the King of Denmark, for example, so they were continually paying Danegeld, or making payoffs to be left in peace, and the Vikings continually broke their promises to do so.

Because the Vikings had attacked the Frankish Empire 10 years earlier, Charlemagne had already set up a coastal defense, and this worked to successfully resist an attack in 820, but could not hold against repeated attacks by the Vikings, so when Ragnar's men invaded in 845, they were met with armies on both sides of the Seine. The king was determined to protect the royal Abbey of Saint-Denis, but the Franks could not mount an effective campaign against the invaders.

The ransom that was paid would be the first of many, and the Vikings, though paid, raided their way back home, pillaging sites all along the coast. And they would return several more times in the 860s, this time against a stronger Frankish defense.

The second Siege of Paris came in 885, this time under the command of Vikings Sigfrid and Sinric, and was a turning point in Frankish history. An eyewitness, a Benedictine monk, Abbo Cernuus, reported that as many as 700 Viking ships and thousands of Viking men arrived demanding tribute, but were denied by Count Odo of Paris. This is the largest number recorded, and although it was given by an eye witness, it may be an exaggeration. This is based on the fact that 700 ships would have carried 50,000 men or more and could have easily taken the city without much of a struggle.

Bella Parisiacae urbis (*Battle of the City of Paris*) is an epic poem written by Abbo Cernuus (Abbo of Saint Germain), who resided at the Abbey of Saint-Germain-des-Pres in Paris. The account is written in quarto, and he recounts the second Seige of Paris in this summary:

"In the year 885... [in] the rich kingdom of the Franks, dazzling like a queen over all cities, renowned for your harbor, much praised

by others, come those that covet your wealth. The river stretches out. To your right and to your left, on your banks are bridges that hold back the waves, and here there are towers that guard the bridges.

"I saw everything and am astonished that no one has spoken of this. Now here are the gifts the cruel ones brought to offer you: Seven hundred high-prowed ships and very many smaller ones, along with an enormous multitude of smaller vessels, the very ones that in the vulgar tongue are often called barques."

William Falconer's Dictionary of the Marine defines a *barque* as "A general name given to small ships: it is however peculiarly appropriated by seamen to those which carry three masts without a mizzen topsail." Barques were considered the workhorses of sailing ships and they could operate with smaller crews. They had fewer square sails and could generally outperform the larger schooner, were easier to handle and went against the wind better than a fully rigged vessel.

Abbo Cernuus continues:

"The deep waters were so overly crowded for a distance that extended more than two leagues downriver that one asked in amazement, where had the river vanished? It could not be seen, hidden as though by a veil of fir, oak, elm, and alder, each one entirely drenched by the water, and when in two days these ships made landfall hard by the city, Siegfried did make his way to the great hall."

Here, Siegfried makes his plea to the bishop for men to defend the city, who vows to guard it, that the city must not suffer destruction, but rather be preserved.

"When dawn had nearly faded, the battle began. Jumping into their boats, the Danes headed for the tower and began to hurl stones at it and riddled it with arrows. The bridges swayed and everyone rushed about trying to

help defend. It was then that Count Odo did shine, and the stalwart abbot, Brother Ebolus, at that place where he was hit, struck down by a sharp pointed arrow. For many, it was the last moment of their lives and others dealt with their bitter wounds and forced the Danes back.

"Fear seized the city and battle horns resounded. Christians fought among the warriors; blood gushed and flowed, darts, stones and javelins were hurled by ballistae and slingshots. And victorious Odo fortified those who were exhausted, rushing about on the tower, and he served them up with oil and wax and pitch in a hot liquid on a furnace which burned the hair of the Danes and made their skulls split open. Indeed, many died and the others went and sought out the river."

This is only a small portion of the riveting account of the events that went on for many months, so long in fact, that some of the Vikings actually went off to other raids and came back to continue fighting. Although historians disagree as to the number of ships in this formidable seige, the fact that they went on as far as the eye could see and blacked out the river paints a vivid picture.

Paris at that time was on an island, what is now Ile de la Cité. It had two low-lying foot bridges which could block ships from passing, and this is where the importance of this town lay. Even the shallowest of the Viking ships could not pass. The success of the Norse raiders in France had always depended on the systemic weaknesses of its rulers; a lack of centralized command, the inability to raise a permanent defense force, and the readiness of its leaders to buy off the Vikings. Now these bridges were fortified with two towers guarding each bridge, and it seemed that Count Odo had marshaled his forces.

This time the Vikings used siege engines to break the city walls. These were constructed of wood and could launch large projectiles, usually enormous stones, like missiles into the walls.

They also tried fire and battering rams, but were met with a mixture of hot wax and pitch. They failed to break the city walls.

The attack was renewed, this time from all sides. They sent missiles into the bridges, launched a ship at them, attacked by land and tried to surround the bridge tower, sent fire by siege engine into the city and tried to set fire to the bridges. They camped outside the city for months, filling the river with debris, plant matter and the bodies of the dead. They set ships on fire and sent them into the bridges. Finally, a hard rain came and the weakened bridges gave way.

That summer, the Danes made a final attempt to take the city, but were scattered by the Imperial Army led by Charles the Fat, which had arrived to aid the Parisians. However, Charles had no intention of fighting. He made a strategic move when he allowed the Vikings to leave, paying them off and letting them sail further up the Seine to Burgundy, a state that was in revolt against the king, and which he hoped would be weakened by the Viking raiders. By paying them a ransom, he angered Odo and his men as well as the Parisians who had fought for nearly a year.

The Iberian Peninsula

At about the same time Harald Blue-Tooth was ejecting Erik Blood-Axe from York, other seafaring Vikings were making their way to Muslim Spain and Portugal on a quest to investigate the territory and wealth of that land.

The caliphs of the 8th century had created an empire that extended from the borders of China to the Atlantic Ocean, from the Sahara to the Caspian Sea, and from India to al-Andalus (Spain), and most of what we know about the encounters between Vikings and Arabs in the territories bordering on the east and west of the Muslim empire is derived from books written about routes connecting the empire.

In the east, the term *ar-Rus* is used to describe Scandinavians the Arabs met in Russia, and in Spain and Western Europe, the term *al-madjus* is used. They were thought to be fire-worshippers, like the Persian Zoroastrians.

"Their religion is that of the Magi, and they burn their dead with fire. Nothing seems more important to them than fire, for the cold in their lands is severe. [These are] the Magus who are [also] called Rus."

The Vikings had been known to do mercenary work, and one 13th century historian, Ibn al-Atir, noted that "*the al-madjus force came to the aid of Alphonse II, king of Galicia, during his campaign against the Arabs in 795*", but the raid on Seville is generally regarded as the start of the Iberian Viking Age. Others believe these were heathen Basques and not Vikings at all, because the Vikings had not yet fully established themselves in the north, what would have been the natural staging ground for entry into the south. Still others believe a description of Charlemagne's distress as he sat at supper "*watching a small fleet of longships carrying out a raid on the harbor*".

The first large-scale incursion came in 844 when a Viking fleet came by river through the Frankish empire to the border between Christian Europe and Muslim Spain. They were roundly defeated in this attempt, but returned a few months later with a fleet of 80 ships that "*covered the sea like dark birds*". Varying accounts claim the Vikings were engaged in sea battles in the harbor at Cadiz near Lisbon for 7 to 13 days. Some made their way inland up the Gualdalquivir River to Seville and established a base, killing or taking hostage any who had not already fled the city. The Viking invaders were eventually defeated in this attack – killed or driven back. Abd al-Rahman II, the presiding emir of Seville, then built an arsenal and a fleet of warships of his own along with a chain of lookout posts along the Atlantic.

Ironically, trade and diplomatic relations took place between the Arab and Viking worlds for several years, and there is little record of Viking attacks between 844 and the next Viking raid in 859, when 62 ships went through the Strait of Gibraltar and looted the port city of Algeciras in Cadiz. This time, however, the Guadalquivir was too well guarded to permit a forced entry further inland. The Vikings continued on and bad weather drove them to Morocco, then they raided their way through the Mediterranean islands and the Italian cities of Luna (now Lucca) and Pamplona.

The leaders of this expedition are believed to have been Hasting (Hastein) and Bjorn Ironside, a son of Ragnar Lothbrok. Hastein thought that Luna was Rome itself, and wanted to sack the city that was the very heart of Christianity, so he employed the familiar cunning tactic of playing dead that had been used before by other heathens, including the Danish king, Frodo, and Harald Hardrada.

He pretended to repent for his evil ways and allowed local Christian leaders to baptize him. Then he instructed his men to report that he had died and ask for a proper Christian burial within the city. Once inside, it would have been a simple matter for him and his men to massacre the innocents. The city was indeed plundered. Unfortunately for Hastein, it was not Rome, as he had thought.

The Arab records that talk about the Viking raids beginning in June 966, a century after the previous round of raids, as alarmingly as the Anglo-Saxon and Frankish chroniclers, with prayers to Allah to destroy them and other outbursts of pious despair.

They inhabited the area of Galicia for 3 years, roaming the city freely as any inhabitants would, and were eventually removed by the troops of Count Conzalo Sanchez. A fourth and final wave of Viking attacks involving Olav Haraldson, the future king of Norway, came in 1008 and lasted until 1038.

But there were other encounters by Arabs with Vikings that were not violent, and chroniclers gave us something that is missing from the accounts of ferocity and bloody battles, kidnappings, raids, ransoms, and beheadings of holy officials. These were generally encounters of trade. The Vikings were viewed as merchants more so than warriors, and were associated with business rather than battle.

One man who observed the Vikings with interest was Ibn Fadlan, who gave an account of the funerary rituals of the Vikings, and another, geographer Ibn Rustah, traveled to Novgorod with the Rus and noted his impressions of the people and their home.

"I have seen the Rus as they came on their merchant journeys and encamped by the Volga. I have never seen more perfect physical specimens, tall as date palms and with ruddy complexions. They do not wash themselves after defecating, urinating or having sexual intercourse. Their day begins with a slave girl bringing them a pitcher of water in which each washes his hands, face and hair, then clears his nose into the water. The process is repeated until all have used the same water in the same fashion. With the Volga flowing nearby, it is a wonder at the necessity of this economy."

"Perhaps it is a bonding ritual to strengthen the loyalty among them, for if one group of them is challenged to war, they all join in force. They stand firm as one man against their enemies until they have won the victory over them."

Ibn Rustah wrote:

"*The friends of a dead warrior dig him a grave resembling a large house and place him in it, along with his clothes, his gold arm bands, food, drink and coins. His favorite wife is buried alive with him before the grave is closed.*"

This is a practice called *sati* or *suttee*, in which a widow throws herself on her dead husband's funeral pyre, but there is no evidence in any of the Scandinavian texts that the Vikings practiced this. The Arab writer likely confused the slave girl, who volunteered to be sacrificed with her master, for a wife.

"They have their wizards [priests], who decide on what they own as though they were their masters, and tell them to sacrifice to their creator whatever they decide of women, men and cattle...and are compelled to carry out their decisions. The wizard then takes [the sacrifice] and hangs them from a gallows until dead."

The writer, because of the extreme cultural differences, has likely misinterpreted the rituals of this alien people, and throughout his writings, seemed inclined toward sensationalism.

A Viking presence never took hold in the south, in Arab lands, in Russia or in what is now Spain, but the trade they encouraged was no doubt a valuable contribution to the further development of these foreign lands as well as the northern countries they dominated.

Chapter 5: Viking Ingenuity: The Shipbuilders

The people of Scandinavia lived among many coastal waterways, with navigable fjords making their way inland. These extensive waterways made it almost compulsory for men to learn how to build ships to navigate their way around the islands. And so it was that they became skilled at ship building, a craft that would serve them well, for their ships were not only strong, they were flexible, two qualities that would allow them to cross the great sea – the mighty Atlantic Ocean.

"The wave beats the high benches; the keel cleaves the wave. The ugly sea will break the beautiful ship, for the sea threatens and the monster weakens the hearts of many. Yet the serpent will not yet come until world's end by Odin's word, and yet our best weapon holds against the elements."

When we think of Viking ships, we think of long boats with high sails and curving ends, perhaps with dragons carved into them, and these were indeed the images that were seen when they invaded, filling the sky with brown sheets painted with their banner. But the Scandinavian people had more than one kind of ship.

Knörrs (*knarr* or *hafskip*) were built for trading. They were slower than the longboats and were built for carrying passengers and cargo. Longships were for exploring and for long voyages. A *frekar* or dragon ship was a longboat used only to invade. The major difference between the *knarr* and the *frekar* was that the longship was fitted with oars and rowlocks and had a low freeboard. This is the distance from the waterline to the upper deck or the height of a ship's deck above the water level. It's measured at the lowest point where water can enter the boat. In contrast, the *knarr* was powered by sail alone, had a high freeboard and only a steering oar.

It's speculated that *knarrs* were also used as troop transports. When piracy landed a great haul that may have filled the warship, these smaller boats could have been used as escort vessels. They were highly maneuverable and could carry armed men, therefore dealing with the problem of counter attacks without sacrificing the number of warriors who could fit on the warship. But they were generally meant for quiet waters such as the fjords and coastlines of Denmark and Norway.

Karvi (karve) – The smallest vessel in the longship category, with fewer than 13 benches, one which is too small for military use. It was a general purpose ship used for fishing or trade with a length to width ratio of approximately 4.5:1. The Gokstad, unearthed in 1880, is an example of a 9th century *karvi.*

Snekkja (snekke) – Snekkja means "thin and projecting". This would have been the smallest longship used for military purposes. It would have at least 20 rowing benches, a length to width ration of about 7:1, could carry 40 oarsmen, and would draw on 1.5 feet of water. These boats were sent out by the hundreds, sometimes in fleets of up to 1,200 ships. They were light and fast and could be easily beached or carried.

Skeid (skeið) – The word means "that which cuts through water". These were larger warships with greater than 30 rowing benches. In 1962 and again in 1997, ships of this type were unearthed in Denmark; the *Skuldelev 2* built circa 1042 measured 98 feet in length and could carry 70-80 warriors. The *Roskilde 6* was 121 feet and dated to around 1025.

Drekkar (frekkar) – There have been no archeological finds of these dragon ships, so information about them is taken from the ancient literature such as the *Saga of Rollo*. They are said to "*ornately decorated*" with grotesque beasts, dragons and snakes likely intended to intimidate and strike fear in their opponents, and were "*used for raiding and plundering*". The Vikings believed these creatures also protected the ship from dreadful sea monsters, so they may have had some other ritualistic purposes outside of making the Vikings fearsome.

However we think of the Vikings and why they began their sudden and dramatic raids, all sources agree that the Viking longship was an incredible piece of technology. There's little debate about their importance in making these raids possible. These dragon ships could travel across vast distances of open ocean waters, and because they were light, very shallow-draft boats, they could easily navigate tiny inlets and rivers. Not only were they light and easily navigable in shallow water, they were fast, so they worked well for traveling up rivers. They could battle stormy seas and be hauled up on the beach where warriors could disembark swiftly, then board as quickly as they came if necessary. This is why the Vikings were such feared pirates. They could attack places where no one would ever think a sea-borne raid would occur, in places that no conventional ship could maneuver.

In the late 19th century, three astonishing discoveries of Viking Age longships were made. In 1867 in the rural southeast end of Norway, a boat named the *Tune* was unearthed from a burial mound and dated to be about 900 years old. A rectangular chamber behind the mast held the remains of a man, a horse, sword, spears, and a saddle.

Thirteen years later in 1880, also inside a mound, the *Gokstad* ship was found. A 2007 medical examination revealed that the remains found in the grave chamber were of a man estimated to have been in his forties. He was believed to have been extremely powerful and muscular at about 6 feet tall – 6 inches taller than the average men of his time. His thigh bones weighed 30 percent more than average, suggesting he spent much of his time on horseback, and he is believed to have died from four wounds from three different weapons: a blow from a sword to the left leg just below the kneecap, a blow to the same knee with a club hammer, a stab wound in the right thigh, and the slicing off of his right ankle.

He was found buried with 12 horses, 6 dogs, 1 peacock, 5 beds, 3 small boats, a bronze pot with a suspension chain, a barrel, buckets, and 64 shields with traces of yellow and black paint that appear to have been fastened to the outside of the ship's rail. The tent shaped grave chamber itself was constructed of notched logs, proving that the Vikings had knowledge of this form of woodworking.

The *Oseberg*, the third ship, was discovered in 1904 and was even more richly furnished. This mound had the unusual distinction of being unrelated to the local tradition, however, and was found isolated in a low-lying area rather on higher ground as most burial mounds were.

Because of the other discoveries, there was a heated attempt by locals to dig around mounds, and in 1903, artifacts were found by a farmer, Oskar Rom. He took them to the curator of the Museum of Antiquities and two days later, the site was visited by experts.

The mound was in excess of 8 feet high and 131 feet in diameter, but it's believed it has collapsed over the years as earth does, with the original height being estimated at 21 feet. In it were two women, one of which is believed to be the slave of the mistress, small axes and knives (no weapons), cooking equipment a whole ox, beds, white woolen blankets, down quilts, clothing, pots, buckets, a weaving tablet, and many other items, all of which had to be carried, along with the boat, over ground to be buried. Outside the grave chamber were a carved ceremonial wagon, 3 sledges with shafts which indicated that they were to be pulled by 2 horses, a gangway, oars, rigging, rope, 5 metal rattles, a saddle, combs, and wooden buckets, 5 dogs, 2 more oxen, 15 decapitated horses, furniture, bundles of unfinished oars, tools, and carriages. It's estimated that the process of moving the ship to the mound and loading all the goods and animals may have taken as much as four months.

The range and quality of intricate carvings, bronze figures, animal shaped head posts, and valuable and ornate gifts all point to a culture that was deeply devoted to their clans, leaders and gods. The discovery of the *Oseberg* was essentially a time capsule from the Viking Age, free from the constructs of novelists, painters, tapestry artists, and clergy.

Construction: Tools, Wood, Cloth and Iron

It's believed that boat builders worked in pairs; a master craftsman and an apprentice who mirrored his work on the opposite side. Tools were mainly chisels, hammers, axes, and hand drills that rested against the breastbone as the handle was turned. Most of the work was done with a long handled cutting axe, a tool that's heavier than a hand axe. They also used a broad edged bearded axe or *skeggöx* to arduously shave and shape the boards.

Oak, ash and pine were used primarily and ships were built from the outside working inward, instead of using the skeleton first method. They chose the clinker style in which each board overlaps the one below it rather than fastening planks edge to edge. Logs for ship building were split with a club and wedge along the central pith rays, in the direction of the wood fiber, then split further into as many as 32 parts. This preserved the fiber so the penetration of water was vastly minimized. It also made the boat light and flexible, but strong, the qualities that gave the Vikings an extreme advantage over conventional warships.

On the *Oseberg*, instead of nails, wood fibers were used to bind shipboards to the interior struts, giving the hull remarkable flexibility.

In areas where a curve was needed, such as the keel and hull, trees were selected that had naturally occurring curves, and selecting these trees was done by the skill of masters. The naturally curving timber gave up to twenty times more resilience in the planking than boards that would have been sawn into the desired shape, and because the keel could not be jointed, the length of the timber dictated the length of the boat.

Each ship required at least fifty cubic meters of oak, and trees often needed to reach diameters of at least one meter or 3 1/4 feet. The average length of a ship was about 57 feet or more (17 or more meters) and about 8 1/2 feet wide. Hulls, with their overlapping planks, were held together with iron rivets and tree nails.

A treenail is what we would today call a dowel or peg. They were used to fasten two pieces of wood together, thus eliminating the need for too many metal nails that would rust. Caulking was done with moss and tar.

Foxtail wedges were used to expand a dowel's outer edge, making it wider at one end. This method secured the trennel in place. When water caused the boat's wood to expand, treenails or trennels would actually make the planks tighter as they absorbed water.

A different type of construction, something called mast-fish construction, held the mast. This was a type of socket construction that allowed the mast to be lowered and removed when not required. When sails were not being used, removing the mast would lessen the ship's drag and increase the speed that could be obtained by rowing.

Sails were rectangular and made of wool reinforced with leather bands. A shield rail ran around the railing of the ship which allowed the Viking shields to be stored in place. This display of shields also created a protective wall and gave an impressive appearance, one that might strike further fear into those who viewed the approaching ship.

Longships were high at both ends, and fighting ships were without benches. Crews would have used their sea chests to sit on. A small longship would have had 13 pairs of oars and room for 30 warriors. Even when fully manned, these boats would have drawn only about 1 1/2 feet of water or 50 centimeters.

A modern replica of the Viking warship *Skuldelev 2,* believed to have been built around 1040, was constructed in 2004 using authentic Viking shipbuilding techniques. It took 27,000 man hours to construct using 14 mature oak trees that measured 3 feet in diameter. The trees were split with axes, not saws which would have been quicker, but which would have destroyed the grain and fibers of the wood by cutting across it rather than along it. This was one of the key factors in the success of these ships.

Planks were overlapped (clinker built) and supported by internal ribs, and the ship proved seaworthy, making a successful voyage across the North Sea in 2007.

Navigation

One of the characteristics of the longship was a steering oar mounted at the rear on a small shaft on the starboard side that acted like the stern mounted rudder of a modern boat, but because it was not stern mounted, it may have contributed to the shallow draft of the ship and would have enabled navigation in almost any type of water.

Fully extended at sea, the oar hung vertically below the level of the ship in a leather strap and could be adjusted up or down to allow for the depth of water. It could be stored horizontally when traveling in shallow waters or prior to landing on a beach. It also allowed the boat to be dragged inland or towed up narrow rivers where there was no possibility of turning around, a feat that would be impossible for a ship with a rudder mounted on a sternpost.

The longboats could be out to sea for days without keeping sight of any coastline. That was a whole new way of thinking because most seafaring people stayed fairly close to a coast so they could keep their bearings. When crossing the open sea, the Vikings used dead reckoning, observing the latitude and longitude so they would have some idea of the distance traveled.

To reckon latitude, they used a sun shadow board – what we call a sundial - a wooden disc with a pin or gnomon (projecting piece) at the center that could be adjusted up or down according to the time of year. It was floated in a bowl of water and the shadow of the sun at its highest point – high noon - was noted.

If the ship was on course, the shadow would reach a circle marked on the board. If it passed the mark, the ship was north of latitude; too short and the ship was south of latitude.

The Vikings carried portable wooden sundials which helped them on clear days, but there might be several days when the sun was blocked out by a thick layer of clouds, fog and mist, so how did these seafaring people manage to navigate millions of miles of open unfamiliar water when the sun wasn't shining? This was a question that had baffled historians for some time, and the alleged mythical tool that was used is believed by scientists to be some sort of natural crystal which the *Sagas* refer to as a sun stone.

Many accounts of Viking sea adventures talk about extraordinary crystals that helped warriors locate the sun and navigate in low light. These "sunstones" or *sólarsteinn* as they were called allowed navigators to pinpoint the sun even when it was hidden by dark clouds and fog, and these crystals are what helped establish them as superior explorers.

"The skies were spitting snow and the king asked Sigurd to locate the sun through the impenetrable haze. He took the stone and looked through it to the heavens where no light came, but from there he could see the invisible sun behind the overcast skies."

In 1967, a Danish archaeologist deduced that these sunstones or navigating crystals were possibly cordierite or Icelandic spar, which would have acted as a natural polarizing filter. He theorized that they could have very easily located the sun by pointing a crystal toward the sky and rotating it until the light passing through it reached its brightest point. Even though scientifically this is true – crystals can indeed polarize light - archaeologists have thus far not been able to find anything resembling the mythic navigational tool among relics at any of the unearthed Viking sites.

Recent research, however, from the University of Rennes in France has turned up Icelandic spar, a transparent variety of calcite, on a 16th-century Elizabethan ship, and this suggests that the Vikings did indeed make use of this same "technology".

Another group of scientists out of Eötvös University in Hungary has recently done testing using a polarimeter to determine the degree of polarization of light filtered by calcite under a range of weather conditions, and their reported findings were unexpected.

"To our great surprise, the patterns of the direction of polarization under totally overcast skies were very similar to those of the clear skies."

The Visby Museum on Gotland, Sweden, houses a collection of 30 lenses of rock crystal dating from the very late Viking period. Testing has revealed that they have imaging powers as good as those of modern optics. They appear to have been turned on a lathe and could have been used as magnifiers, fire starters, to cauterize wounds, or to make up the light chain in a telescope. This is the only find of its kind and it's thought they are not the work of Viking craftsman, but might have come from the advanced workshops of ancient Persia.

Regardless of their methods, the Vikings would have had to be knowledgeable about the major landmarks observable on longer voyages, the direction and strength of currents at sea, sea birds and their environments and flight habits, cloud formations, the use of day and night sky (astronomy), and weather patterns.

Chapter 6: Viking Exploitation: The Traders

The Vikings were on the cutting edge of human exploration. They were looking for opportunities. They were looking for a way to expand their land, their reach, their riches, and their trade networks, and they explored all the way from the heart of Russia to the New World.

There was nothing to lose and everything to gain by being adventuresome because of their beliefs in predestination. They believed that the moment of your death was chosen for you at the moment of your birth. And if it's not your day to die, it didn't matter what you did, who you battled or why you were there. It was either your day to die or it wasn't, and so they had no fear of adventuring into the unknown.

Vikings earned their reputation of the savage warriors that we know them as because of their raids and their attacks on the coasts of England, Ireland, Wales, and France, but their reputation as savages overshadows the contributions they made to cross cultural development throughout this period in Europe.

They built trading towns that ultimately turned into medieval Europe's big cities; Dublin, Ireland, for example, was a trading town started by the Norsemen, and towns along the Volga River, in Normandy, France, and in much of what is now modern Russia.

Walrus tusks and furs were no doubt valuable and rare commodities to take to market in the Arab world, for example, and the sale of slaves was an important source of income for the Vikings.

Rus women wore a band of silver, copper or gold pinned to her bodice, and its size was determined by the wealth of her man. They also wore gold and silver rings, each ring representing 10,000 dirham or Arabic coins. The status of the dirham was a universally accepted currency, in much the same way the American dollar is today, and these coins have been unearthed in great volume across the Viking world, from the northwest of England to the northeast of Sweden. The fact that so many of these coins were buried suggests that the Vikings had reached the status where money was now a surplus.

The Vikings could get into a boat and sail through vast stretches of ocean, making contact with people in foreign lands, and initiating trade communications either at home or with towns along their routes. This was a new thing for a lot of Europe, and the Vikings helped connect the world in ways it had not been connected before.

The Volga Route

The Volga River is the longest river in Europe, running 2,300 miles from the Caspian Sea in southern Russia, closely passing by present day Moscow, to St. Petersburg, just a few miles from the Gulf of Finland. In a continuation of rivers, tributaries and short portages, the Vikings were able to trade all along this route; silks, spices and silver, slaves, furs, wax, amber, and honey in European Russia and Bagdad, and crucible steel swords forged in the Islamic world, where the art of forging had become advanced.

The connection of waterways gave them access to the Byzantine Empire (Roman Empire) farther south, where they obtained wine, fruits, jewelry, fine fabrics (brocade), spices, glass, icons, and books.

"Wooden boats came down to Constantinople from outer Russia; some came from Novgorod, some from the walled town of Smolensk and from Lyubech and Chernigov and from Vyshgorod. All these come along the River Dnieper and converge on the fortress of Kiev.

"The Slavs, who are bound to pay the Rhos tribute, hew the hulls in their wooded hills during the winter, and when they have them ready, at the seasons when the frosts dissolve, they bring them to the lakes nearby. Since these discharge into the River Dnieper, these people come to the Dnieper, make their way to Kiev, drag their ships along for fitting out and sell them to the Rhos.

"The Rhos buy the plain hulls, and from their old ships, which they break up, they supply oars, rowlocks and whatever else is needed. So they move down the Dnieper in June... [And] on the island of St. Gregorios they sacrifice live birds because of the huge oal that stands there."

As small international trading centers grew, merchants were attracted from all across Europe, the Arab states and Asia, with many of these centers being Norse trading centers, settlements and navigational ports of call. But perhaps the most significant trade center begun by the Vikings was Dublin.

Dublin

This is the city where Thorgils the Devil took his stronghold and created an entrenched Viking settlement. It grew to major proportions and became one of the most important ports of call for Viking ships. Here, the Norsemen returned with goods to trade: timber from Vinland; walrus, ivory, furs, skins, and wool from Greenland; fish, animal fat, wool cloth and clothing, sulfur, and falcons from Iceland; tin, wheat, honey, woolens, silver, barley, and linen from England; slaves, furs, wax, and honey from Russia; silks, fruits, spices, wines, gems, silver, jewelry, and brocade from Italy and Greece; weapons, jewelry, wine, glass, salt, and wool cloth from the Franks; soapstone from the Shetland Islands; timber, iron, soapstone, whetstones, barley, and tar from Norway; iron and furs from Sweden; and amber, slaves and furs from the East Baltic.

It's believed that at some point, Norse traders were not made up as much by warriors as they were by farmers, merchants who were not professional "Vikings". Since trade was done by barter, the traveled with their goods so they could personally verify the quality and quantity of goods received in trade.

Journeys made for the sole purpose of trading consisted of those who brought goods to trade, who paid for their passage with trade and who were allowed a certain amount of space for his goods, equal to anyone else on board except the ship's captain. All traveling traders were obliged to crew the ship and pull the ship on shore or portage it since there were no professional crewmen aboard. They were also required to pay a harbor tax, and in exchange, they could store their goods.

Gold and silver were also used to trade or barter, using weights and scales to measure them. If a length of gold or silver was more than was needed, it was cut into pieces. When the Arab silver mines were depleted, silver was obtained from Germany.

It was natural for towns to begin popping up around these routes, and professional craftsmen and smiths also came to sell their skills for repairs on boats, shoes, clothing, and any number of other necessities.

Houses were erected, roads were put in place, and towns and settlements might be seasonal or permanent.

The New World

The Graenlendinga Saga, composed in the twelfth century, documents the discovery of North America. Nearly one hundred years later, *Eirik's Saga* gives us a version of the same event, but both indicate that Erik the Red founded an Icelandic colony in Greenland and that his son, Leif Erikson (Leif the Lucky), in an attempt to extend the Greenland colony across the Davis Strait, discovered the land known as North America five hundred years before the Italian born Christopher Columbus sailed across the Atlantic Ocean in Spanish ships. No one knows who wrote these two Icelandic Sagas, but it's in these writings that we get our first real record of the people who lived on the Eastern shores of the

North American continent in the eastern portion of Canada, what is now Nova Scotia.

Leif Eriksson had actually started out in an attempt to explore the uncharted land encountered quite by accident by Bjarni Herjólfsson. He sailed south, following the same route as Herjólfsson, and planned to exploit the natives, but what he encountered makes for one of the most fascinating stories in the history of exploration.

Three distinct regions of the journey after the crossing of the Davis Strait were named, each one reflecting the topography of the region. Helluland, which translates roughly as "land of rocky slabs, was what is believed to be Baffin Island. Sailing south, they reached Ungava Bay in Labrador, which they named Markland. Following the coastline further brought them to the Strait of Belle Isle where they went through the channel between Labrador and Newfoundland into the Gulf of St. Lawrence, and this is where they established the settlement of L'Anse aux Meadows.

About 150 radio-carbon dated items have been made on the three residential halls unearthed in L'Anse aux Meadows in 1914, and about one third of them have been found to be connected to the period of Norse settlement there, dating between 980 and 1020. The buildings were on scale with the largest of Icelandic halls, built of turf with timber roofs, and on a terrace up from the shoreline.

There has always been some controversy regarding the landing location of Leif Eriksson and his crew and how far they traveled. In the 1980s, some strands of cordage were found at an abandoned settlement at the northern tip of Baffin Island in Canada, the area believed to be where Leif Eriksson landed. The strands were not consistent with the twisted string from animal sinew made by indigenous people. They were made from the long hairs of the arctic hare. Under a microscope, it was discovered that the hairs were actually spun into soft yarn then woven into the cordage, and there has never been any evidence showing that indigenous tribes were spinners or weavers.

The samples were shown to an expert on Viking textiles, an archeologist from Denmark, who confirmed that they were exactly like strands of yarn made by Norse women in Greenland.

In the area settled by ancient inhabitants, known today as Nanook, a green hollow or valley lays among freshwater ponds and is filled with thick spongy moss. The greenery is perfect for turf, one of the essential elements the Vikings used in building construction. The protected cove is perfect for Viking ships, and the boggy patches contain bog iron, something Viking smiths were skilled at working.

A team of archeologists revisited the storage rooms at the Canadian Museum of Civilization and found more spun yarn that had come from what are now Nunguvik, Tanfield

Valley, Willows Island, and the Avayalik Islands, making up more than a thousand miles of coastline. They also found other items that would have been distinctly Viking: wood (the landscape is treeless), tally sticks used by Vikings for recording trade transactions, spindles, traditional Norse whetstones, several carvings of what looked like European faces with long noses and beards, and whalebone with auger marks. Indigenous people had no drills.

But the Sagas describe bad relations between the Norsemen and the local inhabitants, whom they referred to as *skraellings.* These tribes had been initially fascinated with the color red the foreigners were able to achieve in their woolen cloth, but disagreements broke out and there isn't much documentation beyond this other than a few small ships going back and forth to Greenland. It remains a mystery why the first settlements in the north did not survive.

Chapter 7: Viking Home Life: A Democratic People

Norse society in Iceland was without warlords or kings. Life was about feasting, farming, the power of chieftains and the church, marriage and the role of women, but it was also about blood feuds. Local courts favored compromise over violence, however, and the independent state of these medieval people was a prototype for a democratic society. This is in stark contrast to what we may have believed and our long held perceptions of the Vikings and their way of life.

The ideals of the heroic life included the obligation to the social group, loyalty and rewards, but this was the privilege of the upper classes. Not everyone could take on the adventures we hear most regarding the Viking heroic cult. We often think of these ruthless people as carousing into the night and perhaps drinking to excess, but ordinary people behaved differently. Aside from the warrior class, they were not much different than us.

"A man should not hold on to the ale cup, but drink moderately from it. Spare of speech he should be, or silent. No man will accuse you of ill manners for going too early to bed."

The Vikings were suspicious of clever or learned people. They believed it was possible to know too much. Perhaps it was their belief that the gods were the only ones who should be so wise.

Archeological finds indicate that the average male in Norway was about 5ft 9in in height, and the average female about 5ft 3 in.

Clothing was made from wool, leather and linen, with metal fastenings. Spinning and weaving were common.

Dental remains show almost no caries (cavities) in stark contrast to today's society, but their teeth were much more worn, likely due to chewing on bones or using teeth as tools.

Food was what we might expect: wild game such as bear and elk, domestic animals such as sheep and hogs, fish that could be dried, salted or smoked, milk and whey, and anything they could forage including mushrooms, grasses and nuts.

Milk was soured and used in bread. Most often, meats were boiled, not roasted, and made into something called *skause*, a dense broth of meat, vegetables and perhaps tree bark in which meat was cooked, then removed and eaten and new meat was added to the old broth.

Cultivated vegetables included white carrots, cabbages, peas, and greens. Foraged foods included wild apples and berries, herbs and spices such as mustard, horseradish and cumin.

Despite having such a healthy diet, however, remains have shown that these people suffered from intestinal parasites, possibly because of unsanitary conditions in storage of perishable foods.

Skeletal remains indicate that some did live into old age, well into their 80s, and suffered from degenerative joint disease (arthritis), and according to the sagas, other conditions common to old age, such as failing eyesight and hearing loss, were experienced.

Other skeletal remains show horrific battle injuries such as the top of a skull cut off by a sword. In one man, the imprint of ring mail could be seen clearly on a femur bone, showing that the force of the blow to the leg was so severe, it caused the mail to go through the muscle to the bone. But it was a severing of the spine by a sword to the neck that killed this man.

But there was still some honor in battle. According to the sagas, if fights continued for a great length of time, both sides would stop to allow men to bind their wounds so they could continue fighting.

"The men examined their wounds to determine the extent of their injuries. One examined the snow where an enemy had lain, put it in his mouth and realized it was blood from an internal wound. He knew the man would soon be dead and there was no need to chase him."

Medicine

The literature tells stories, which perhaps are highly embroidered, that talk of a man whose shoulder was sliced to the lungs and the lung fell out. He was protected by his men and healed over the summer to fight another battle. Another was severely wounded having his foot cut off at the ankle, but he rose and killed his attacker then continued to fight. The stories may or may not be exaggerated, but there's no doubt the Vikings had some medical skills, however limited.

Medical arts were practiced, but the custom of using chants and charms was common. Runes were often inscribed on whalebone and placed under one's bed to cure an ailment. If the ailment wasn't cured, they believed the runic inscription was wrong and would be rewritten.

Magic could also be used to prevent a wound from healing, and it was believed that a sword wound, for example, would not heal unless it was rubbed with the sword's own healing stone. Injuries received could be healed by reddening a hill with the blood of a sacrificial bull, making a feast of the meat for the elves who lived there.

Herbal remedies were known, according to the ancient texts, and other remedies included lancing, cleaning wounds, anointing, bandaging, setting broken bones, cauterizing, bleeding, and midwifery.

Religion

The *Book of Settlements* names several Norwegians who were baptized in Iceland, but once they were gone, their children reverted to the practices of sacrificing to Odin and Thor. By the second half of the 10th century, however, the religion began making its way into Denmark, the Scandinavian Peninsula and among ordinary Icelanders.

Thor was still the most popular of the gods and this was the god heathens looked to in their struggle to resist the demands of Christianity. A war of words among poets began, with the heathens mocking Christians for their lack of manhood and the Christians mocking the heathens for their superstition. Thorvald the Far-Traveler, a companion of Olaf Tryggvason, is said to have been one of the first missionaries to preach the gospel in Iceland, and Olaf is attributed with the conversion of Norway, Iceland, Shetland, Orkney, and the Faroes.

In a verse by a woman poet named Steinun, we see how superstition played a part in the lives of the Icelanders. She writes about the displeasure of the Aesirs (gods) over the Christian presence and their destruction of a ship at sea:

"Thor drew Thvinnill's animal, Thangbrand's long ship, from land, shook the prow's horse and hit it, and hurled it against the sand. On sea, the ski of Atall's land will not

swim henceforth, for a harsh tempest sent by him has hewn it into splinters.

"Before the bell's keeper, bonds destroyed the beach's falcon, the slayer of giantess-son broke the ox of seagull's place. Christ was not watching when the wave raven drank at the prows. Small guard, I think, god held, if any, over Gylfi's reindeer."

Society

Viking society was ruled by the law book known as the *Grágás*, which provides a wealth of information about how they lived, and which had very specific rules for the formal rights and duties of free men and women, their behavior and activities, appearance, and the punishments that went with breaking the laws. Here are some examples:

One will be held blameless who bleeds or cauterizes someone for the good of their health.

A man who has been injured is entitled, if he wishes, to avenge himself up to the time of the *althing* where he is required to pursue the case for the wounds.

Women are prohibited from cutting their hair. (This was considered a masculine trait and was a privilege reserved for men only. Generally, men did not wear tresses, with few exceptions).

If a man goes berserk, the penalty is lesser outlawry, and the same is for them who accompany him, except if they restrain him.

If a man climbs on the back of a man's horse without permission, he incurs a fine. If he rides away, he incurs a payment of three marks. If he rides as far as past three farms, then he causes fines to be incurred along with outlawry.

Women

"In woman's words let no man trust nor what a wife may say. For their hearts are formed on a whirling wheel and fickleness is fixed in their breasts."

Feuding and lawsuits were primarily carried on by men, and women were primarily viewed only as they relate to men. Despite the fact that a freeborn woman could legally run a farm, she was not allowed to take part in the workings of the judicial system or in neighborhood panels (local government). Only men served as judges in the assemblies that took place in spring or in *althing* courts, and men as young as twelve years of age who could earn their own keep were allowed to participate in local government.

If a woman had a grievance, she must put her intent to prosecute into the hands of a man. The idea was to distance women from the inevitable violence that took place as prosecutions moved through the stages of threat to force.

Women were barred from carrying weapons.

A woman who had reached the age of 16 (20 in some places) could choose her place of residence.

A woman was to be punished the same as a man if she kills a man or woman, or causes injury.

Even though women were viewed as second class citizens, they were protected. There were penalties of lesser outlawry for the seduction of women, from kissing to full seduction, including putting on her headdress.

Marriage

Marriage was considered a bargain made between two families. A bride purchase was made and the bride price was paid, agreed upon ahead of time. If a man initiated a divorce, the woman had the right to retrieve her bride price.

Women could initiate divorce for the following reasons: when her husband wanted to take her property out of the country against her will; when violence had been committed; for incompatibility; or when the husband wore feminine clothing.

Marriage required that the marrying couple own in common 120 legal ounces of silver, plus their everyday clothes, and they must have no other dependents. Fortunately, not everyone abided by this law or the descendants would have been far fewer. It would have taken a landless worker almost 20 years to amass just the minimum amount required for legal marriage.

When Christianity took hold, a new marriage law was written. According to the Church in Rome, a couple must not be fewer than 7 degrees apart in family relations. In 1215, this was lowered to 4 degrees because the restriction made it difficult for some to find partners.

Status

Viking society was hierarchical, but it was possible for one to raise his social status. At the top were the rulers who controlled the land and the wealth, and above them were only the kings and earls.

Armies were led by these aristocrats and were made up of free men or *karls (karlr)*, middle class working men and small landowners who were allowed to carry weapons. These men were also entitled to attend *althings* or assemblies. They could vote and contribute to decisions about the community.

Most 'vikings' never went to battle and only a small relative number were professional warriors. The Great Army was manned by these professional warriors who may have been in service for 15 years, but this was the exception, not the rule.

Women were generally treated as subservient in the society, but as part of the family structure, they were much loved and valued. They could also achieve high status. If there were no male heirs, they could inherit family wealth and land, and if their status was high enough, there might be an inclination to allow them some political influence.

"Ragnhild was like unto her father, Blood-Axe, killing her husband Arnfinn Thorfinnsson Orkneyjarl, a son of the Skull-Splitter, and marrying his brother, the Earl of Orkney, Håvard Thorfinsson, whom she also had killed in order to marry their last brother. In this, she had the capacity to scheme and murder like her father."

At the bottom of society was the slave class. Slaves or *thraells* had no legal rights but were important to the economy. The Vikings were considered to be some of the greatest slave traders of their time. Slaves could be moved, and movable wealth was what they wanted.

Women were taken from raids and either killed or taken as prisoners and sold as slaves. But there was a process in place whereby a slave could be freed. The slave owner had to agree and the slave had to buy him off, a seemingly impossible task.

Building Construction

Finding the archeological remains of turf buildings is difficult because the remains are covered by windblown soil or destroyed by erosion, but what has been located has revealed that two kinds of turf were used for building: marsh turf from swampy ground and dry grassland turf. Marsh turf has been slower to decompose in the cold damp climates and was common in Iceland and Greenland. This was also the type of construction found in the Canadian-Arctic settlements.

Turfs were cut into several shapes, with the most customary being long flat rectangular strips and blocks that could be used to form strong well-knit walls more than 3 feet thick. The blocks and pieces had to be cut and carried to the site, then they were laid two deep with a gap in the middle that was filled with soil. The blocks that formed walls were laid in a pattern in much the same way a bricklayer staggers bricks rather than laying them directly in a vertical row. This added additional strength.

Roofs and rafters had to be strong enough to withstand northern gales, so rafters were divided into two parts, with the middle ends resting on bracing beams. Pieces were connected with pegs, notches and other wooden joinery, and sod was used to cover the frame. The weight of the roof was divided into upper and lower roof loads by a triangular support system that rested on long vertical pillars and took the weight down to the dirt floor, where a flat stone was placed under each post to keep it from sinking and to protect it from moisture rot.

In the 11th century, longhouses were built with four rows of internal supporting pillars which moved the roof weight from the turf walls and allowed the addition of new internal rooms that connected to each other.

Viking Runes and Stones

"Listen, ring-bearers, while I speak of the glories in war of Harald, most wealthy."

When we think of the Vikings, we may think of them as barbarians who were uncultured, and we certainly do not see them as scholars or literary masters, but they did express themselves in writing in the form of the sometimes puzzling symbols known as runes. Thousands of inscriptions in stone, wood and metal have been unearthed, and each item gives us a glimpse into a culture who believed in the power and protection of the gods, telling fortunes and casting spells, and the glory of war.

"Let no man carve runes to cast a spell, save first he learns to read them well."

The *Furthark* is the runic alphabet, but its origin is unclear. Some believe it came from the Latins since that was the language of commerce during the Roman Empire, and Germanic tribes would likely have had contact with merchants, thereby exposing them to the language. Others think the Etruscan alphabet is the more likely origin based on proximity, the early 2nd and 3rd century dates of many inscribed artifacts and the many similarities of letterforms in Etruscan and runic alphabets.

The Scandinavians tell it differently:

"Odin speared himself to a tree so that he could receive the knowledge of the script. Suspended for nine windy nights, he learned their mysteries, and these he passed on to his people. The gift from Odin is divine and possesses magical powers. With great reverence they must be used to honor the heroes and to make powerful the implements of our daily use; the box and the comb, the hilt and the scabbard."

The actual name is simply made up from the first six letters (f, u, th, a, r, k) in the same way the commonly used modern alphabet is made up of the first two letters of the Greek alphabet, alpha and beta.

Each "letter" or figure is called a rune, and it has a phonetic sound, but similar to the

Chinese alphabet, it also has a distinct meaning, and these meanings are directly linked to Norse mythology. Like any alphabet, runes were used as a means of communication. At some point, however they became magical and were used for divination and other mystical purposes. Here are the translated meanings of the Elder Furthark rune symbols:

Fehu: Cattle, gold, or wealth in general.

Uruz: Strength, speed, and good health.

Thurisaz: The giants of Norse mythology.

Ansuz: Any deity, but particularly Odin.

Raido: Signifies a long journey.

Kenaz: A torch or some other source of light.

Gebo: Denotes a sacrifice to the gods.

Wunjo: Comfort, joy, or glory.

Hagalaz: Hail as in weather or hailing projectiles such as in battle.

Nauthiz: Need or necessity.

Isa: Ice.

Jera: Year or harvest.

Eithwaz: Yew, a sacred tree used to make rune wands.

Perth: The meaning and/or translation of Perth remains unknown.

Algiz: Defense, protection or self-preservation.

Sowilo: Sun.

Tiwaz: Tyr, the God of War; often carved on weaponry.

Berkano: The birch tree, associated with fertility and Idun, Goddess of Spring.

Ehwaz: Horse.

Mannaz: Mankind.

Laguz: Water.

Ingwaz: Reference to the Danish hero Ing or to the Danes in general.

Dagaz: Day or daylight.

Othila: Inheritance or the passing on of property or knowledge.

Rune stones are simply boulders that were naturally roughly shaped, so the inscription went over a fairly uneven surface. They were inscribed to tell stories of events or in memory of someone, raised as a monument to the dead similar to the tombstones we use today. They are typically pagan, but the use of them was taken over and expanded when Christianity took over.

In central Sweden alone there are several thousand rune stones, most of which have a cross in the middle or some other symbolic image such as a mythical beast or dragon, and an inscription written in a ribbon-like carving that runs around the stone in varying fashion. Typically, the inscription asks for God to aid the soul of the dead person, along with the name of the person who raised the monument.

Other rune stones are memorials that tell a compelling story, generally memorials to war heroes. The inscriptions are often poetic and sometimes it's difficult to discern their meaning, likely because of the vocabulary, the change in the meaning of words over time and the language itself.

"Thorulf erected this stone, Svein's retainer, in memory of Eirek, his comrade [comrade in arms], *who met his death when fighting men besieged Hedeby, and he was a ship's captain, a very good man."*

Runes are written from right to left, and were mostly used between the 9th and 13th centuries, but continued in Scandinavia through about the 17th century. There are at least 3 main varieties noted by historians.

Early: (also called Common, Germanic or Teutonic) Used in northern Europe, it had 24 letters and was divided into 3 groups of 8 letters each.

Anglian: (Anglo-Saxon) Used in Britain; letters were added to represent the sounds commonly used in the Old English; it had 28 letters; after 900 AD, it had 33 letters.

Nordic: (Scandinavian) used in Scandinavia and Iceland; instead of adding letters to represent the rich sounds of the language, they compounded letters so that a letter might stand for more than one sound; the furthark was thereby reduced to 16 letters.

There were variants of the Nordic script that included dotted runes (*stungnar runir*), the greatly abbreviated Hälsinge runes, and Manx runes used on the Isle of Man. It's believed that the Isle of Man was seized and occupied by Viking warriors who then intermarried with local women. Man remained an independent state until 1266, and today still has independent status, with its own parliament, the Tynwald. This is a direct throwback to the *althing*, and comes from the word *thingvollr*, from *thing* (assembly) and *vollr* (field).

There are greater than 4,000 surviving runic inscriptions and manuscripts, with more than half coming from Sweden. The remainder are from Norway, Denmark, Britain and Ireland, with some found in France, Germany, Russia, and surrounding islands.

Burials

At the beginning of the Viking Age, all Scandinavians were considered heathens, but by the time the period ended, the Scandinavians considered themselves to be Christians, and the long thread of religious and cultural change is evident throughout the Viking Age, as seen in the crosses on many rune stones. But the Vikings still buried their dead with what they felt was necessary to honor them. For example, women were buried with jewelry, gold brooches, necklaces and rings, shears and combs, while men were buried with weapons including spears, swords and scabbards, axes, and shields.

Women were also buried with keys to show they were household managers. Metal fastenings such as pins, buckles and strap ends were found, indicating that people were buried fully dressed, the natural fabrics of their clothing having long since disintegrated. Graves were always oriented to the west.

Burial mounds were large barrows under which some prominent or important people were buried, and entire ships were sometimes buried under these mounds.

Vikings are always associated with ship burials, but ships were very expensive to build, so only the elite class or those of great importance, such as chieftains and kings or women of high status, were buried in ships or had elaborate mounds built around their graves.

These laws about ship burials are taken from an account of the Danes written in about 1200, but they're corroborated by archeological findings, down to the size of the ship and the status of the individual buried in it.

The head of a family was to be buried with his horse and weapons.

The bodies of 10 captains might be burned together in one ship, but the body of a commander had to be burned on its own on a pyre in a ship.

A king or an earl who fell in battle had to be burned in his own ship.

"They led the slave girl to a thing that resembled a doorframe. She placed her feet on the palms of the men and they raised her up to overlook this frame. '*Behold, I see my father, and my mother. I see all the line of my family seated with my master in Paradise and Paradise is beautiful and green; with him are men and servants. He bids me come to him.*' And so they brought a sacrificial hen; she cut off the head and threw it away, then they took the hen and put it into the ship."

Recent forensic testing of the two women found buried on the Oseberg suggests that both women lived in Agder in Norway, home of Queen Åse, the mother of Halfdan the Black and grandmother of Harald Fair-Hair. One of the women is believed to be Queen Åse, a very high status lady. She wore a fine red woolen dress with a pattern that indicates wealth, and a fine white linen veil. The other woman had a plain dress of blue wool with a wool veil, indicating she may have been a companion or servant sacrificed to keep the other company in death.

The grave had been robbed of most of its valuables, but the robbers had left four elaborately decorated sleighs and a richly carved wooden cart with four wheels, the only complete Viking cart found thus far, as well as a brass bucket with a handle in the shape of a figure sitting cross-legged that is compared to the Buddha sitting in the lotus position. The design is of Celtic origin, however, indicating it is an image of the Iron Age god, Cernunnos.

Other aristocrats were buried in wagons, and many smaller boats have been found in burials, but no burials have been found in large trading vessels, indicating that merchants, although they may have been wealthy and influential, were not entitled to ship burials.

The poor created *skaeiths*, symbolic "ships" made by forming stones in the shape of a sailing vessel. They believed them to be equivalent to real ships in their ability to carry their loved ones to the afterlife. At Lindholm Høje in the Danish portion of Jutland, a remarkable Viking burial ground contains 200 such "ghost ships", each with a rune stone as the "prow".

At Lake Tissø in Zealand, Denmark, within a kilometer of what was found to be a royal residence, numerous objects were found in the water such as axes, spears, swords, and jewelry. These numbers indicate that the objects were deliberately thrown into the waters as part of a ritual common to ancient practices. There are examples all over Europe of this, where precious objects were offered, and many date back three thousand years to the Bronze Age.

But at Lake Tissø, the significance is believed to be tied to the god Tyr, from the word *ti*, an Old Danish word meaning "god".

Within the complex at Lake Tissø, in the residence, were found the remains of many horses, animal skulls and limb bones of animals, suggesting that they were also used for sacrificial offerings, a practice that went on throughout much of the 9th and 10th centuries.

Chapter 8: Norse Mythology

"King Bylfi visited three of the gods to question them about the origins of the world and he learned that everything began in an empty chaos that contained a world of heat and light called Muspelheim, and an opposing, dim, dark and cold world called Nifelheim. The two worlds were separated by a great chasm called Ginnungagap, which bore a great giant named Ymir who was nourished by the primordial cow, Audhumla. And so it was that the salty stones around her became Buri who fathered Bur who wed the giantess, Bestla. From her came Odin and his brothers who killed Ymir and created the physical world. They flung his parts and blood about to make the sea, the land, the mountains and cliffs, and the vault of the heavens."

When the Vikings first settled in Iceland in the 9th century, they brought wooden carvings of their Norse gods with them. Their devotion to Odin, Thor, Freyr and Frigg was deeply embedded in their society, and Viking warriors went to battle knowing that the gods would protect them. If they fell on the battlefield, they would be rewarded with admission to Valhalla.

Paganism was rampant in Iceland until around A.D. 1000 when lawmakers agreed to make Christianity the country's official religion, and the gods of the Vikings were driven underground. The religion was never fully forgotten, however, thanks to the writings of 13th-century Icelandic scholar Snorri Sturluson, He recorded the ancient Nordic mythology in *The Prose Edda*, sometimes referred to as *The Younger Edda* or *Snorre's Edda.*

"In the beginning, before the heaven and the earth and the sea were created, the great abyss Ginungagap was without form and void, and the spirit of Fimbultyr moved upon the face of the deep, until the ice-cold rivers, the Elivogs, flowing from Niflheim, came in contact with the dazzling flames from Muspelheim. This was before Chaos.

"And Fimbultyr said: Let the melted drops of vapor quicken into life, and the giant Ymer was born in the midst of Ginungagap. He was not a god, but the father of all the race of evil giants. This was Chaos.

"And Fimbultyr said: Let Ymer be slain and let order be established. And straightway Odin and his brothers—the bright sons of Bure—gave Ymer a mortal wound, and from his body made they the universe; from his flesh, the earth; from his blood, the sea; from his bones, the rocks; from his hair, the trees; from his skull, the vaulted heavens; from his eye-brows, the bulwark called Midgard. And the gods formed man and woman in their own image of two trees, and breathed into them the breath of life. Ask and Embla became living souls, and they received a garden in Midgard as a dwelling-place for themselves and their children until the end of time. This was Cosmos.

"The world's last day approaches. All bonds and fetters that bound the forces of

heaven and earth together are severed, and the powers of good and of evil are brought together in an internecine feud. Loke advances with the Fenris-wolf and the Midgard-serpent, his own children, with all the hosts of the giants, and with Surt, who flings fire and flame over the world.

"Odin advances with all the asas and all the blessed einherjes. They meet, contend, and fall. The wolf swallows Odin, but Vidar, the Silent, sets his foot upon the monster's lower jaw, he seizes the other with his hand, and thus rends him till he dies. Frey encounters Surt, and terrible blows are given ere Frey falls. Heimdal and Loke fight and kill each other, and so do Tyr and the dog Garm from the Gnipa Cave. Asa-Thor fells the Midgard-serpent with his Mjolner, but he retreats only nine paces when he himself falls dead, suffocated by the serpent's venom. Then smoke wreathes up around the ash Ygdrasil, the high flames play against the heavens, the graves of the gods, of the giants

and of men are swallowed up by the sea, and the end has come. This is Ragnarok, the twilight of the gods.

"But the radiant dawn follows the night. The earth, completely green, rises again from the sea, and where the mews have but just been rocking on restless waves, rich fields unplowed and unsown, now wave their golden harvests before the gentle breezes. The asas awake to a new life, Balder is with them again. Then comes the mighty Fimbultyr, the god who is from everlasting to everlasting; the god whom the Edda skald dared not name. The god of gods comes to the asas. He comes to the great judgment and gathers all the good into Gimle to dwell there forever, and evermore delights enjoy; but the perjurers and murderers and adulterers he sends to Nastrand, that terrible hall, to be torn by Nidhug until they are purged from their wickedness. This is Regeneration.

"These are the outlines of the Teutonic religion. Such were the doctrines established by

Odin among our ancestors. Thus do we find it recorded in the Eddas of Iceland."

Yggdrasil: The Tree of Life

Yggdrasil is an eternal green ash tree with branches that stretch out over all the nine worlds and extend up to the heavens. It's carried by 3 enormous roots; the first going to Asgard, the home of the gods; the second going to Jotunheim, the land of the giants; the third going to Niflheim where the dragon, Nidhug, gnaws on the root and sucks the blood from the dead bodies.

At the top of Yggdrasil lives the eagle who is the bitter enemy of the dragon, and running up and down the tree is the squirrel Ratatosk, who does what he can to antagonize them against each other.

The First War of the Gods

"At one time, the gods lived in harmony, each with his special gift, and the golden era of the world was without malice. The Æsir, the gods and goddesses of war, and the Vanir, the fertility gods, played in the meadows together, listening and talking and enjoying the blessings of Yggdrasil."

"One day the seer and enchantress, Gullveig, came to Odin with talk of gold, for this was what she lusted after, and the Æsir speared her for her greed, for they loathed such things. They burned her and she emerged unscathed from the fire; thrice did they burn her, yet she lived, and the Vanir swore vengeance against the Æsir. And so the war between the gods began."

"Asgard and Vanaheim were battle raged, but each was equal to the other, and so an exchange was made in truce that Freyr and Freyja of the Vanir should live in Asgard, and Hoenir and Mimir of Vanaheim should go to live with the Vanir. Thusly was the golden age of the gods ended."

Ragnarök

Ragnarök is the end of the world; the day of doom for the gods and humans; the final battle between the Aesir and Jotuns.

"The fimbulwinter will cause a 3 year frost to cover the land, upon which there will no longer be vegetation, and animals will die from the bitter cold. The sun will be covered with gray clouds as thick as the sheep's wool and the all-knower will warn the giants that Ragnarok has begun; then will be warned the gods and all the dead."

"Brothers will kill brothers; a horn will sound loudly, the warning from Heimdall will blow, and this will be the battle at the end, the day that all the Vikings will pick up their swords and armor to fight side by side with the Aesir."

"The giant, Surt, will set the world on fire and the mighty Midgard serpent will emerge from the sea and engulf the Vigrid plains, spraying poison and causing destruction."

"The sun and moon will be swallowed by wolves and Yggdrasil will fall to the ground. Odin, too, will be killed by the Wolf, and Thor and the Serpent will kill each other. Finally, an inferno will cause the world to sink into a boiling sea."

"And then shall a new world rise from the sea, shimmering with green and gold, and the two who were left behind in the battle, the man and the woman who found sheltering in the sacred tree, will emerge and repopulate the land. Modi and Magni will inherit the hammer of Thor, their father; Vidar and Vali and Honir will sit in the throne of Odin, their father; and in Idavoll they will build a new house with a roof of gold, for they are the only gods now."

"And there will be a new place called Okolnir where it will never be cold though it is in the mountains of Nidafjoll. And the shore of corpses that greets the screaming north wind shall have walls made of writhing snakes and a pit for thieves and murderers who will be the food of Nidhug, the great dragon."

Chapter 9: The Viking Gods of Valhalla

Like many early civilizations, the Scandinavians believed in many gods, and the cosmological world was conceived as a flat circle that was divided into three distinct regions that shared a common center. The innermost world was Asgard where the Aesir lived. Odin lived in Valhalla, Thor lived in Trudheim, and Freyja lived in Folkvang.

Beyond the inner region of Asgard where the Aesir lived was Midgard, where humans dwelled. It was believed to be located midway between the gods in Asgard and Utgard, or the outer place, the outer rim of the world where giants lived along with other elemental beings associated with untamed chaos. Between Utgard and Midgard was the sea.

There are hundreds of gods and demigods in Norse mythology, and they were believed to be mortal, just like humans. They could be captured, killed or tricked, and hoped they would live long enough to see Ragnarok.

Odin

Most of what we know about Viking religion comes from the poems of the *Poetic Edda* and the *Prose Edda*, which describes Odin as "*the highest and oldest of the gods.*" This is the Norse god of war and poets; the father of the battle-slain. His role was to inspire great oratory and to give fighting men courage in battle. He ruled over poets and warriors.

"*He rules all things, and however powerful the other gods are, they all serve him as children serve their father. Odin is called All-father because he is the father of all the gods; he is also called Valfather because his chosen sons are all those who die in battle. Valhöll* [Valhalla] *is for them.*" The word *valr* means "the slain" or "those slain in battle."

Odin was the "god of the hanged", also called the "helmeted one." He had two pet ravens, Huginn (Thought) and Muninn (Memory), which embodied his function as the god of wisdom.

Numerous prophesies in the Eddas tell us that the monstrous gray wolf, Fenrir, who is destined to be the death of Odin, will feature prominently in the last battle of the gods and men against monsters and giants – the Battle of Ragnarok.

“And Odin, with his eagle and his helmet and his spear in hand, will ride Sleipnir with the enormous army of Asgard and will go with all the gods and brave *einherjar* to the battleground.”

Thor

A son of Odin, he’s responsible for natural phenomena such as wind, rain, thunder and lightning, and ruled over farmers and the common man. He’s associated with oak trees and is often remembered for his famous magical hammer, belt and iron gloves.

Thor is believed by some to be the most powerful of the gods, and he appears in the *Prose Edda* predominantly in a protective role. An idiosyncrasy of Thor is that he is vulnerable without his hammer. People wore amulets or pendants in the shape of Thor's hammer that invoked his protection.

"I am the god of War, the Thunderer in the northland, my fortress, and I will reign forever; here amid the icebergs I will rule the nations. Miölner the Mighty is my hammer, and there is none among the jotuns and sorcerers who can withstand it. I hurl it far off and it returns to me, redoubling my strength."

"The light of the heavens, in flashes of crimson, you may behold, and it is I, Thor, with my red beard blown by the night wind, affrighting the land. My eyes are lightening and the wheels of my chariot are thunder. My hammer rings in the earthquake!"

"For it is by force that the world is ruled, and strength alone is triumphant. This is Thor's-

Day! Thou art a god, too, and thus single-handed unto the combat, gauntlet here, I defy thee!"

Baldur

A son of Odin, he was the god of the summer sun, said to be so bright that light shone from him. His mother was the goddess Frigg who had a dream that foretold of his death, and through the trickery of Loki, Baldur was indeed killed by a spear made of mistletoe.

"Most beloved Baldur, most joyful, who makes the gladdened heart, my dreams have been ominous for your grave misfortune. And it was Odin who mounted Sleipnir and rode to consult with the seeress, and when he reached that cold and misty world, he found a feast in honor of his son, Baldur."

"The consulter of the dead was merry for this prophesy, and Odin returned to Frigg, who would make that no harm came to her son, so she secured the oaths of all living things that her son should not be harmed. And Loki, the trickster, saw an opportunity for mischief, knowing that the mistletoe was yet left to swear its oath."

"And so it was that Loki tricked the blind Hodr to throw the shaft of mistletoe which killed the joyful god."

Freyja

She is the goddess of love and fertility, and the embodiment of female sexual power; a sorceress who is skilled at *seiðr* (say-der) meaning "snare". This type of magic is particular to Norse mythology and gave the ability to change the course of destiny set forth by the three Norns.

"She entered into the prophetic place, where all thought is fluid, and roamed the Nine Worlds, traveling in spirit, seeking to change the curse on the Hard One, for she saw his end in Stamford Bridge. And in the secret mind, where there were luck and healing for the sick, control over the storms of Thor and calling for the food of the forest, there could be found no false future for Hardrada. He would be first maimed in his manhood, his men pushed back by the enemy, and the battle lost in the river, with his head split asunder and the blood of his family spewed across the plain."

Freyr

He is the brother of Freyja and the god of male potency, good weather, good harvests, and fertile beasts; he is the son of the sea god, Njörd.

"In Ragnarok did Freyr fight the fire-giant, Surt, with a stag's antler, for he was without his magic sword which he had given to Skimir, his shield-bearer. He was the first to be slain at the end of the world, yet he was the bright slayer of Beli, the giant; he was Beli's bright slayer."

Loki the Trickster

He is the blood brother of Odin and the son of giants who was adopted into the family of the Aesir, and who brought trouble everywhere he went. He is a mischief maker and the god of wildfire. He is evil at heart, cunning and without loyalty. He is also a shape shifter who might appear in the form of a water creature, human, insect, or animal, and he is the cause of the death of the god Baldur.

"Loki came from the giants and was unlike the other gods, for he seeks only to cause mischief among gods and men. He looks for trouble and redoubles it in trickery. Now he is evil and wears the blood of Baldur; by the troll woman are his offspring, the wolf Fenrir, and the serpent of Midgard and Hel, the goddess of death."

Aegir

Aegir is Lord of the Sea and one of the three jotuns who lived in Asgard. He predates the Aesir and Vanir and lives in the coral caves under the sea. He is the brother of the wind and fire.

"A great feast was in his hall, Brime, where the drinking horns filled themselves by his magic and all the gods did eat of his bounty. In Aegir's hall they ate from the shifting sand and the watery billows and glassy brine; from pearl shells they ate sea flowers and dew; the tides were above and below but the winds and waves were absent."

Hel

She is the daughter of Loki who became queen of the underworld known as Niflheim. She rules over illness and the sick bed, old age, misfortune, hunger and starvation. At the gates of Hel stands Garmr the Hel Hound, who will signal any new arrivals, and the dragon Nidhug will then suck their blood so they may easily join the army of the dead. When Ragnarok arrives, the end of the world, this army will attack the humans in Midgard.

"From the high hall of Hel were raised the wolf Fenrir and the serpent Jormungandr, and the prophecies spoke of their disasters, so that Odin called for them and threw the serpent into that deep sea that lies round all lands."

"And from this place, the goddess of death did visit Baldr in a dream and, standing at his side, declared that in three days' time she would clasp him in her arms. And so it was that in three days, the mistletoe which caused his wound would bring his end."

Valkyries

The Valkyrie in Norse mythology are the daughters of Odin, and they appear continually throughout the Icelandic sagas, in the *Poetic Edda* and in runic inscriptions. There seem to be an undefined number, with many names appearing in the poems.

These female supernatural creatures are associated with fate. They choose those who will be slain in battle and then escort them to

Valhalla, home of the gods, ruled by Odin. They also appear in the text as the lovers of heroes and other fictitious mortals, and may be accompanied by ravens, swans or horses.

They are called wish maidens, choosers of the slain, maids, and wish fulfillers and are often conflated with other spirits: Norns who spin the threads of life, and Dísir, the guardians of individuals.

"The great King Haakon made his final request as he lay on the battlefield, that, dying among the heathens, he should be given a burial place as seems most fitting. And so he died on the same rock upon which he was born and was greatly mourned. His finest clothing and armor were laid with him and the words were spoken according to the custom of heathen men, and so he went on his way to Valhalla."

"For who should be chosen among those in battle to dwell with Odin in Valhalla? Those who see Göndul leaning on her spear shaft or sitting gratified on horseback are goodly bidden home, for they are worthy for the gods to grant it and they shall ride forth to the green homes of the godheads."

Norns

There are 3 Norns whose names are Past, Present and Future and they are also goddesses who spin the threads of life and decide the fates of men. They are responsible for bringing water to the Yggdrasil, the Tree of Life at the center of the world.

"And so to respect the goddesses and gain favor for the child, porridge was given to the newborn babe, that he might have long life, good health and prosperity."

Jotuns

Jotuns are giants with superhuman strength and were considered to be the first living beings.

"Ymir, the first of the living, was the origin of the world, and his home was Jotunheim of the Nine Worlds, where he ate of the fish from the rivers and streams, and from the forests, he took the animals for food, for the land was not yet fertile."

It may be difficult to understand a strong faith that revolves around this type of thinking, but the Norse believed in their religion in the same way the religions of today hold their followers. Even among Christians, Nordic beliefs in elves, trolls and nature spirits were handed down from generation to generation, and a modern group of followers have revived these ancient gods once again.

The Asatru Association was formed in Reykjavik in 1972, and received recognition from the Icelandic government as an official religious organization. In 2012, construction began on the first temple in more than 1,000 years to honor the ancient Norse gods. At a cost of nearly $1 million dollars, the 4,000 square foot temple will exist in harmony with the natural rock of the hillside and is expected to be completed by the end of 2016.

Admittedly, the ceremonies and rituals of the Asatru Association "do not read the medieval texts literally and eschew a strict interpretation of Norse mythology for its more spiritual qualities." Instead, they view the ancient text as poetic metaphor for human nature. It seems that some people love the appeal of their Viking roots and "really want to go back to the Viking era."

Chapter 10: Viking Creatures of Magic

The Medieval Age was replete with its share of fascinating mythical creatures that influenced the daily lives of people. They were mischievous, dangerous and magical, and each had their place in Viking lore.

Dwarves: Dwarves were believed to be created from the maggots living inside the bodies of giants.

Dain the Dwarf made the cursed sword that must slay a man before it can be returned to its sheath. Anyone hit with this sword would die or suffer a wound that would never heal.

Fafnir the Dwarf is the son of the dwarf king magician, Hreidmar and is the guard of his father's house.

"One day, Loki was traveling with Odin and they were captured by Hreidmar. Loki was forced to turn over a ransom of red gold, and

Fafnir killed his father to get the gold for himself. His greed grew so great that he became a gold hoarding dragon, whom Sigurd heard of. Sigurd made his way to the house of Hreidmar to obtain the treasure, but a dragon had taken it, which was Fafnir, and it was stored in the lair of the beast. Fafnir warned Sigurd that any man who should steal the treasure would die, but Sigurd knew it was the destiny of man to live ambitiously and that he would die someday anyway. To this end, he killed Fafnir the Dwarf/Dragon, seized the gold and ate the heart of the dwarf."

Hit the Ogre: Hítardalur was a big farm and ancient church in Mýrasýslu in the Hitardalur valley. Legend says that the ogre, Hit, and a half human-half ogre named Barour Snadrellsás were traveling through the mountains returning to their lair, which they must reach before daybreak or they would be turned to stone. They missed their timing and were indeed turned into a pair of very specific rock formations still found to be in that place.

Elves: Light elves were what we might call guardian angels. They are minor gods of nature and have the power to help humans without actually interfering in their lives. They cannot change the course of fate, but they are magical and can inspire humans.

"The white *älvor* appeared by the grace of the god Freyr, clad in silk, and the Dane was raped by her beauty, he that slew in battle all who would come before him with the wielding of his great axe. Yet Eirik fell beneath the elf and they drank together, that he might be inspired in battle."

Dark elves live to annoy humans and make trouble for them. They, too, are magical and are described as being "hideous".

"And so in the night, the dark elf sat upon Ragnar's chest as he slept, and the warrior dreamed of the battle ahead. When he woke, though the sun had not yet risen, dread filled him, yet he knew not why, for his men were readied with armor and supplies and outnumbered the coming forces. He mounted his steed, who reared up as though frightened, and the mist that was *dökkálfar*, the black elf, passed before his eyes."

Cats: Cats were feared and thought to be witches in disguise. The goddess Freya, who is a sorceress, had her chariot pulled by two enormous cats.

"The great forest cats were wild, yet Freya tamed them by her magic to pull her cart, and the *skagcatts* loved her, for she was kind to them and gave those two fish and mead."

Dragons: Dragons were thought to be magical, and there are many in Viking mythology, including Nidhoggr, aka Dread Biter, who lived at the foot of Yggdrasil; the Firedrake of Beowulf fame; Jormundandr the Midgard Serpent; and Fafnir, the dwarf son of magician

Hreidman, who killed his father and was turned into a dragon by his greed.

"The dragon sat at the bubbling cauldron that was Niflheim, at the source of the rivers of the world, and devoured the corpses of the evil-doers, enjoying the taste of the dead, for Nidhoggr was evil itself and destined to survive Ragnarok, the doom."

Eagles: To the Norse, the eagle is a symbol of strength and death.

"And the walls of Valhalla were guarded by wolves and eagles, and in it I saw my place among my people, shields and spears in hand, ready to stand with Odin at Ragnarok, for that land is hallowed, lying near gods and elves, and the glorious eagles."

Wights: These were creatures believed to protect homes, farms and villages. They were spirits with no particular form but were thought to be more like elves than humans, and could be seen only in the right light.

"The *landvætir* were agitated by the pole which Egil set up so that they would go astray, wanting these guardians to confound the king and queen out of the country. And so the spirits went out to the west and north, to the hillsides and hollows, large and small, until the spirits lived there no more and the earth around became a wasteland."

Ravens: These are the symbol of Odin. His two ravens were named Huginn (Thought) and Muninn (mind or memory).

"The birds flew with a message to Odin, from Midgard they came with news for the raven god, for the birds can speak by the magic of Odin. Each day they set forth to fly and each day Odin mourned for their loss that they may not return. 'For Huginn I fear, lest he come not home, but for Muninn my care is more. For Huginn is for the hanged, yet Muginn is for the slain in battle who will join me in the halls of Valhalla.' "

Wolves: Fenrir, Fenrisulfr, Vanagandr, and Hrodvitnir were all names for the famed wolf who would be the undoing of Odin at Ragnarok.

"The beast, the monstrous wolf, the second sorrow, whom I came to strike down and slaughter with my hands and drive through with my sword, into the heart of him, yet the prophecy will stand and he will be my undoing in the final battle. Side by side with Beli's bright slayer will I fight Vanagandr, then shall sweet Frigg fall."

Chapter 11: Viking Heroes and Legends

A hero or legend in Viking lore might not always be a "good guy" in the way we think of legendary heroes today. Generally, the fiercer they were, the more the writers and poets turned them into heroes and documented their deeds.

A *saga*, which simply means *story*, was written as a historical document, more or less, and could have been handed down by word of mouth through generations, or could be a wholly artistic creation. Long epic poems were written in a grand style that exemplified individuals, and both sagas and epics were generally written many years after the end of the Viking Age.

There were sagas of the Scandinavian kings, sagas of the Greenlanders, and Chivalric sagas, among other types. The Icelandic sagas, praising the heroic deeds of members of Icelandic families, are considered to be the highest form of classical saga writing, but the more accurate writings might be those classified as contemporary sagas, which were written in the time period, soon after the actual events occurred.

Then there are the legendary sagas which blend history with myth and paint a picture that is both entertaining and insightful regarding how these people viewed their heroes.

Epic poems are extensive narratives about a historical event, but they may not necessarily be factual. They were often oratory and were handed down by memory, so they changed in the telling over the generations.

Beowulf

One of the most famous and cherished of these stories for modern historians is *Beowulf*, the oldest surviving Anglo-Saxon epic poem written in the Old English. The surviving copy is believed to be from circa 1000 and was discovered in England in the 1600s, but the original was probably composed somewhere between 700 and 950.

Although it's written in the language used by the Anglo-Saxons between 450 and 600 and the story is about the adventures of a pagan, based on references in the text, it was likely written by a monk or court poet with Christian beliefs.

It incorporates components of Anglo-Saxon tradition with Christian moral principles in an extraordinary look at the journey of one man. *Beowulf* emphasizes values that were important to Norse warriors, such as courage, loyalty to one's comrades, and honor for those who fight and die bravely among those for whom fighting was a way of life, and it reflects the warrior culture of ancient Germanic peoples.

Beowulf tells us about a Norse warrior who possessed the strength of 30 men. He rescued Denmark and Sweden from monsters that were terrorizing the people of that land, particularly a monster named Grendel who lurked in the dark swamps of Hrothgar's kingdom.

"Grendel attacked the great hall at night, when the warriors were quieted by drink and much merriment and tales of their victories in battle. In the morning, Hrothgar was assailed with the blood and remains of Grendel's attack and sent up his cries to the heavens."

The next night, Grendel returns and kills again. For 12 long years he came killing warriors and farmers, women and children, and still the attacks did not cease. Prayers for protection did not help and eventually, the great hall was abandoned.

The stories of Grendel's horror went out to kingdoms far and wide, where they reached the land of a man named Beowulf, one who was renowned for killing great sea monsters and giants in the hills and caves of Sweden. His skill and courage in battle caused him to be thought of as a hero of the people, so he sailed to Denmark to rid them of the monster, Grendel.

"Fourteen brave men did he take on his ship, and at Heorot he was much welcomed by Hrothgar. A great feast was prepared in his honor, yet one named Unferth, did not believe the tales of his bravery. 'Had you been as brave as you believe yourself to be, Unferth, Grendel would no longer be terrorizing the land'. In this, the king was confident that Grendel would finally be defeated by Beowulf."

"And so it was that Grendel appeared that night and engaged in a battle with Beowulf, who seized the monster by the arm and ripped it from his powerful body, and he returned to his cave to die. But the struggle was not over, for Grendel's mother vowed revenge."

Beowulf and several warriors track the monster to her lair in the swamps, but she is invulnerable to the swords and weapons of men. A struggle ensues and Beowulf is dragged through the gory swamp to her cave where he sees a mighty sword hanging from a wall.

"He grabbed the sword and with one monumental blow cut off the monster's head. He cut off the head of Grendel's corpse which lay behind its mother, and Beowulf carried the two through the swamp along with the melted remains of the mighty sword that slew the monster. And so he was awarded *wergild* for his bravery and returned with his men to Sweden to become their king."

The practice of offering *wergild* was traditional in early Germanic societies. This was the price set on a person's life based on their value to society. In the event of death, particularly on the battlefield, that person's family would receive *wergild*, and this custom replaced the practice of seeking revenge for the loss of a loved one.

In the second half of this epic poem, even though he is now an old man, Beowulf goes on to slay a dragon that is terrorizing his own kingdom.

"The great dragon slept on an ancient treasure, and when Beowulf's slave came upon it, he thought to steal a golden cup to please his king. But the dragon was cunning and counted his treasure each day, for he was greedy and quick to notice the missing cup. So he flew into the countryside breathing fire and destroying all the homes in the villages."

"And Beowulf took with him to the dragon's lair 11 warriors of great repute, whereby they might slay the beast. But the king entered alone for the sake of his men, and in the battle, was fatally wounded, though the dragon was also killed."

"The great warrior and king, Beowulf, was burned on a cliff overlooking the sea, and the ancient treasure which was locked in the dragon's lair was burned with him in the ceremony to praise him."

Though hundreds of years have passed since the writing of Beowulf, it's still a popular story that reflects all the heroic qualities we expect from an epic adventure. He risks his own life with courage and resolve to save others. His is as fearless as any modern day hero who meets the challenges of his fate bravely, knowing that the memory of his deeds will live on.

If you recognize any of these images from the famed books by J.R.R. Tolkien, you are not mistaken. Much of the tales of *The Hobbit* and the *Trilogy of the Ring* (*Lord of the Rings*) was taken from ancient stories of Germanic, English and Norse origin, including the dragon and his treasure, ancient runic writings (of dwarfish tongue written in elvish script) and giants (orcs, goblins, trolls, and the Balrog). Tolkien ingeniously fashioned his tales of middle earth around Midgard, where humans dwelled, and set them in the Middle Ages, the period in which the Viking Age took place. Even the ship which carried the elves to their homeland in *The Return of the King* was modeled after Viking ships, and the swamp through which Frodo and Samwise must travel on their way to Mordor resembles the swamp at the mouth of Grendel's cave as described in *Beowulf.*

Tolkien interwove many of the dark moods and texture of Viking and Anglo-Saxon poetry into his work. He was an Oxford academic who specialized in early Germanic literature, poetry and mythology, and in philology, which deals with the structure and relationship of languages. The influence of ancient Norse mythology in *Lord of the Rings* is evident.

As a boy, he read and translated the Old Norse language and the *Elder Edda* (*The Poetic Edda*), and these were a deep force in his work. It's well known that he derived the names of the dwarves in *The Hobbit* from the first of the poems in the *Edda*, the *Völuspá* (*The Prophecy of the Sibyl*).

"I don't much approve of The Hobbit myself, preferring my own mythology...to this rabble of Eddaic-named dwarves out of Völuspá, newfangled hobbits and gollums

invented in an idle hour, and Anglo-Saxon runes." (J.R.R. Tolkein)

Although Tolkein took much of his material from the Old Icelandic literature, his work is not to be taken as a direct translation of the facts, but as an entertaining fabrication that mixes language, history, details, and myth into a creative interpretation of medieval times.

Here's a look at some of the prominent and very real Viking heroes, legends and bad guys:

Ragnar Lodbrok: Ragnar Hairy Breeches (circa 745-794)

Known as Ragnar Hairy Breeches, Ragnarr Loðbrók was a Norse king, considered to be a hero. He was the curse of France and England and the father of Ivar the Boneless, Bjorn Ironside, Halfdan Ironside, Halfdan Ragnarsson, Ubba, and Sigurd Snake-in-the-Eye.

According to legend, Ragnar distinguished himself by many raids and conquests, particularly in the first siege of Paris, until he was eventually seized by his foe, King Ælla of Northumbria and killed by being thrown into a pit of snakes. His sons, Halfdan Ragnarsson and Ivar the Boneless, bloodily avenged him by invading England with the Great Heathen Army in what would ultimately be a fourteen year war.

Ivar Ragnarsson: Ivar the Boneless (794-873)

Ivar Ragnarsson, aka Ivar the Boneless, was a son of Ragnar Lodbrok, a Viking warlord of exceptional ferocity and cruelty, and reputed to be a berserker. The Sagas describe him thusly:

"Only cartilage was where bone should have been."

Perhaps this wasn't a literal description, but a way of saying he was extremely flexible. He was reported to be very large, dwarfing other men, with powerful arms able to carry a bow that was much stronger and with heavier arrows.

In 873, the Great Viking Army of Ivar Ragnarsson is reported to have wintered in Repton, England and the *Saga of Ragnar Lodbrok*, Ivar's father, states that Ivar the Boneless was buried in England. During an excavation at the churchyard of St. Wystan's in Repton in Derbyshire, the skeleton of a 9-foot tall Viking warrior was uncovered, and archeologists believe it to be the remains of Ivar the Boneless.

Harald Halfdanarson: Harald I, Harald Fair-Hair (858-942)

Harald Halfdanarson is the tyrant son of Halfdan the Black, and as a boy, he became king after Halfdan's death. Known as Harald Fair-Hair, he was the person who consolidated the territories of Norway into a unified country, making him the official founder of Norway.

"His hair grew thick with a magnificent sheen very much like silk, and he was the handsomest of men, very strong and big of build." He took an oath to not cut, trim or even comb his hair or beard until he became king, and so until then, he was known as Shock-Head or Tangle-Hair.

One of his sons was Erik Blood-Axe and another was Hakon the Good, who both became kings after his death.

Thorfinn Torf-Einarsson: Thorfinn Skull-Splitter (890-963)

Thorfinn Torf-Einarsson was Earl of Orkney in the 10th century and appears briefly in *St. Olaf's Saga.* He joined with Erik Blood-Axe in a raid in England and later, the earldom was weakened by murder plotted among the ranks of the family. The unstable reigns of each successive earl generally ended in violence caused by dynastic infighting.

Egil Skallagrimmson (904-995)

Egil's Saga touts this person to be the greatest Viking bard, a man who was a fierce warrior but who was also gifted with the art of making poetry. Unfortunately, he killed the son of Erik Blood-Axe and was sentenced to death, but because he was able to recite an exceptionally fine poem to King Erik, he was spared execution.

"I dragged my oak ship to sea and loaded my vessel's hold with its cargo of praise, for the great King Erik who escaped the arrow's weaving while other men sank to the ground. In this, Erik won his glorious name."

In another poem he writes:

"I have been with sword and spear, slippery with bright blood where kites are wheeled. And how well we violent Vikings clashed while red flames gorged men's roofs and we, raging, killed and killed."

"Now things go hard with me. On the headland stands the sister of Odin's enemy, yet serene, in good heart and undismayed, I shall meet death face to face."

Erik Haraldsson: Erik Blood-Axe (910-954)

Erik Haraldsson became known as Blood-Axe because of his savage feuding, horrific even by Viking standards, and for the murder of four of his brothers in a bid for his father's throne. He was then usurped as king by his youngest brother, Hakon the Good, and was exiled to England, where he became King of York for a time until he was killed in battle. He was the last Viking king of Northumbria and his death marked the final step toward a united England. His funeral ode describes the preparations for the arrival of King Erik in Valhalla:

"What dream was that, said Odin, when I thought before dawn I was making Valhalla ready for a slaughtered army? I roused my great champions, bade the Valkyries wake, strew the benches, washed out the beer mugs, and brought out wine for a prince who is coming from the world. I await such noble fighting men as will make my heart rejoice."

Harald Gormsson: Harald Blue-Tooth (935-985)

Harald Gormsson was the son of King Gorm the Old and ruled as king of Denmark from around 958 and king of Norway around 970. He is believed to have been forcibly removed from this throne by his son, Swein Fork-Beard. The appellation Blue-Tooth is somewhat of a mystery. Some say he had one bad tooth which was dark in color, others say he wore only blue garments which used an expensive dye to emphasize his royal status.

An inscription on a large stone in Jelling, Denmark (referred to as the Jelling stone, of which there were several) states that Harald turned the Danes to Christianity, and he is also credited with building the oldest known bridge in Scandinavia, the Ravninge Bridge.

Eirik Thorvaldsson: Eirik the Red-Beard (950-1002)

Eirek Thorvaldsson was nicknamed Eirek the Red for his red hair and beard, and was a principal player in the Viking colonization of Greenland. Once banished from Iceland, he spend 3 years in exile, with much of that time being spent exploring the long coastline. When he returned with tales of the land he discovered, he called it Green Land so it would be more attractive to settlers, but the greater portion of this island was wilderness made of rock and ice. With a colony of 25 ships that set sail in the summer of 985, only 14 of them arrived in the new land.

Two settlements were created, one on the eastern shore and one on the western, about 300 miles apart in what is now Qaqortoq and Vestribyggo, and Erik was the chieftain of Greenland where he became respected and wealthy. As the population grew, an infectious disease took the lives of many, including Erik.

Sveinn Tjuguskegg: Sweyn I, Swein Fork-Beard (954-1014)

Sveinn Tjuguskegg, aka Sweyn I Fork-Beard, was another king of Denmark, England and parts of Norway. He was the son of Harald Blue-Tooth and the father of Cnut the Great who led a rebellion against his father, deposing him and driving him out. Because his father had converted to Christianity, he was given the Christian name Otto, but he never used that name, though he may be referred to as Otto in some literature.

There are various accounts of his deeds. Some say he was a persecutor of Christians and others say he was ordering churches to be built in Denmark throughout a 14 year alleged exile, while at the same time leading raids against England.

One thing historians agree on is that he led numerous raids in his effort to conquer England between 1002 and 1012, triggered, they say, by his desire to take revenge for the ethnic cleansing of Danes by the English, an event referred to as the St. Brice's Day Massacre of

1002. Sweyn's sister, Gunhilde, was killed in this massacre and he may have been seeking revenge for her death.

In 1013, he led a full-scale invasion, and an account of the event from the *Peterborough Chronicle* tells it like this:

"Before the month of August, King Sweyn came with his fleet to Sandwich. Very quickly he went round East Anglia into the mouth of the Humber and so upward along the Trent until he came to Gainsborough. All Northumbria bowed to him, as did the people of Lindsey and the Five Boroughs. He was given hostages from the shires, some with his son, Cnut, and they went to Oxford where the town dwellers soon bowed to him and gave hostages. From there he went to Winchester and the people did the same, then eastward to London."

"London put up a strong resistance led by King Aethelred and Thorkell the Tall, the Viking leader now in allegiance to the English, so he went west to Bath, after which Aethelred surrendered and went with his sons into exile."

This final event left the throne to Sweyn and he became the first Danish king of England. Unfortunately, he died about 5 weeks later, perhaps deservedly so. He is reported to have been cruel and brutal, burning women alive and impaling children on lances. But his short-lived reign and then death created extreme political instability in England and left it open to what would culminate in the Norman Conquest.

Leif Eriksson: Leif the Lucky (970-1020)

This is the son of Erik Thorvaldsson (Erik the Red) and he's credited with being the first European to make landfall in North America, nearly 500 years before Christopher Columbus. He was raised in Greenland with his two brothers, Thorvald and Thorsteinn, on an estate called Brattahlid in the Eastern Settlement. From there, he voyaged to Norway, was blown off course to the Hebrides where he spent the summer, then went on to Norway where he accepted the mission of introducing Christianity to Greenland.

He's most noted in the *Saga of Erik the Red* and the *Saga of the Greenlanders* for his famous voyage to Vinland, the name for North America. A merchant named Bjarni Herjolfsson had sighted land to the west after also being blown off course, and later Leif traced Bjarni's trip.

"He purchased Bjarni's ship and with a crew of 35 men, the expedition was organized to set sail to the new land. He landed first at the rocky place of Helluland, the flat rock land [today's Baffin Island, Nunavut in Northeastern Canada] and voyaged on westward to Forest Land [Labrador], and so to the luxuriantly vegetated place where there are many salmon."

He reportedly overwintered there and continued to explore, discovering many vines, giving rise to the name Vinland. He returned in the spring to Greenland with a cargo of grapes and timber.

Soon, other Vikings made their way to the new world. One such expedition was led by Thorvald Eriksson, and in typical Viking fashion, their encounter with the *skroelingjar*, the native people, led to hostility, violence and bloodshed. Because of this, the history of these contacts has been lost. There was no way for the people of that time to recognize that Leif Eriksson had stumbled upon a vast new continent that would one day have global implications.

Christopher Columbus claimed to have visited Iceland in 1477, and it's very likely that this is where he heard of the new world beyond the sea. He did not set off into a void as some history would tell it.

Canute Sweinsson: Cnut the Great (985-1035)

Canute Sweinsson was a prince of Denmark, son of Swein Fork-Beard, and a king of the North Sea Empire which included Denmark, the north of England, Norway, and parts of Sweden, which he acquired after many years of Viking activity in the region. Cnut was notorious for casually leaving hostages after cutting off their hands, ears and noses, leaving the message that the English had broken an agreement, even though that agreement was with Swein, his father, and that since Swein was now dead, they were released from their bargain.

After battling with the English for over a year, most of which was with Aethelred and his son, Edmund Ironside, they eventually agreed to terms. Cnut was to have the north of England and Edmund would keep the south for his lifetime, after which it too would pass to the Danes. Within weeks, Edmund was dead, likely murdered, and Cnut became king of the whole of England for the next 19 years.

One of the benefits of having a Viking king was that he could protect England from Viking raids which had been weakening the country for

30 years. He also married Aethelred's queen, Emma, thereby stopping any challengers from the previous dynasty, and he executed one of Aethelred's sons and forced another to take refuge in Normandy.

He's credited with harmoniously uniting chieftains of Denmark and England without using brutality or force, a tactic he employed to maintain his power over the two kingdoms, but he was also a bigamist, having the queen Emma of Normandy in the south and another, Aelgifu of Norhampton, in the north. This did not sit well with the Catholic Church, so he began to repair all the monasteries and churches that had been damaged in Viking raids and he restored their plundered treasures. Whether he was motivated by faith or politics, he was able to win them over and get important concessions for his people under Popes Benedict VIII and John XIX. He also obtained reductions for tolls his people had to pay on their way to Rome.

Harald III Sigurdsson: Harald Hardrada (1015-1066)

Harald III Sigurdsson, nicknamed Harald Hardrada (hard ruler), is one of the most famed Viking leaders. Before his reign as king of Norway, he took part in the Battle of Stiklestad at the age of 15 with his half-brother Olaf Haraldsson, who was later to become St. Olaf. Olaf was killed as the two attempted to reclaim the Norwegian throne which Cnut Sveinsson had taken two years earlier, and Harald was wounded and went into exile, eventually landing in Russia. He and his Viking contingent were welcomed as mercenaries and were soon employed as protectors of the emperor. Harald rose to commander of the elite Varangian Guard and soon found he had celebrity status.

His reputation now preceded him. The Guard was ordered to man the Byzantine warships and Harald took his men into the Caliphate, where they took eighty Arab strongholds, and then to Jerusalem, where the whole country was given to him.

When he returned to Constantinople, he was accused of holding onto gold that rightfully belonged to the emperor and was subsequently thrown into a dungeon.

"Shortly, a woman with two servants came and let down a rope into the dungeon, allowing Harald and his men to escape. They went forthwith to the palace and killed the guards, seizing the emperor to put out his eyes and castrate him."

Once again, Harald returned to Scandinavia and began raiding the coast of Denmark, where the illegitimate son of Olaf, Magnus the Good, was now king. Magnus was unwilling to fight his uncle and they agreed to share the throne. Conveniently, Magnus was dead a few months later, leaving Harald the sole ruler. In 1066, now virtually a career warmonger, he was killed at the Battle of Stamford Bridge by

Harold Godwinson, the new English king. He was perhaps the last of the great Vikings.

Chapter 12: The End of the Viking Era

"Viking" is a word for which there is no substitute, no synonym. This word alone is the only one that really encompasses the broad category of people, their activities and the events that took place in the 8th to 11th centuries.

Through all the years, the Viking Age is vivid in the memories of many, including our modern history, but history is fluid. It changes over time as our perspective changes and as new information is made available to us. It would seem that the events that happened are unalterable, but the place of the Vikings in history is relative as our values, morals, religions, and societies change and we evaluate things differently.

Today, the Vikings still bring into sharp focus images of a terrifying people jumping from beached longships and pillaging rural communities, yet surprisingly, they are still seen as larger than life, almost heroic people. History has shown us the reasons for this and has justified, to some degree, their plundering rage against what they saw as the destruction of everything they stood for as a people before they were known as Vikings.

The Village of Stamford Bridge: The Last Stand of the Vikings

In September of 1066, England was ready to engage in battle on their southern coast with the Normans who were forming their forces across what is now the English Channel. At the other end of the country, however, a fleet of 300 Viking dragon ships were bearing down on them from the northeast, carrying 9,000 warriors.

One city after another fell before them as they lined up their ships for miles along the riverfront headed by the fierce Harald III Sigurdsson of Norway, aka Harald Hardrada, a Viking who was a practiced warlord with a career that spanned more than 35 years on the battlefield. His main ally was Tostig Godwinson, the exiled brother of King Harold Godwinson. Anxious to take revenge against his brother and return to England, he found a willing conspirator in Hardrada while the unsuspecting English awaited the Normans.

"Many of the commanders of the English armies were green, new to the battlefield. They positioned their men along the road, protected by the marshy ground on their left and the river on their right. When the battle ensued, they hacked their way against each other, shields clashing and blood spewing, fighting for every inch of ground and dying from their wounds."

"But Hardrada proved a battle-hardened foe and his military strategy quickly gained momentum against the English. He swung his troops away from the river and forced his opponents into the marsh where many were drowned or killed by the point of a blade. The marshy flow became halted by the blood and bodies of the English."

"And so it was that the Viking contingent settled on Stamford Bridge to receive their bounty; the hostages, cattle and other goods that were the spoils of war. The Viking leader left his camp with a light group of men and encamped in the meadows near the bridge."

Meanwhile, about one week before the Vikings invaded from the north, the other King Harold, who had been awaiting the Normans, sent the citizen militia back to their shires and had dismissed the housecarls. Housecarls were what we might call mercenaries or professional soldiers. When he was told about the battle up north, he quickly changed his tack and reassembled his forces to several thousand strong.

As he neared the area, he received word that Hardrada and his men were camped within 10 miles of their position. Now his plan was to take them by surprise. At dawn, 25 September 1066, the army departed for Stamford Bridge.

Hardrada's army was indeed taken by surprise. They had accepted their victory and were unprepared for another attack. Having removed their heavy hauberks, they lolled by the river near what is today Battle Flats Farm.

"The Viking sentries spotted the dust rising from the road some miles away, just over the ridge, and they were expecting their spoils to be delivered. The sun flashed off Saxon armor and they quickly realized their error. They raced to prepare for battle, sending scouts to hold back the English, but they were swiftly overtaken."

"Yet one lone Viking defender stood greater than 6 feet tall with broad shoulders and a massive battle axe ready to cut the Saxons down. In this, the Vikings were able to assemble their defense."

"But Hardrada, the berserker, was speared in the groin and the English poured over the bridge. The Norsemen walled themselves with their shields against the onslaught and a savage and ferocious battle ensued, each man slashing savagely amid the fray. The Viking commander fell and the fever of battle caused the warriors to circle their leader in a corpse ring, fighting in a final frenzy."

"The victorious Saxons were merciful, allowing Hardrada's young son, Olaf, to sail home free of ransom. Only 24 longships of the original 300 were needed to carry the surviving Vikings, and the bleached bones of the dead littered the fields of Stamford Bridge for 100 years."

The French, however, led by Duke William II, later styled as William the Conqueror, had been raping the countryside in the south and the Saxons received little rest as they rode to muster a defense, but they were weary and the outcome was not a victorious one for the English. Ironically, many Vikings had pledged their allegiance to the French crown and Normandy had been under Viking control since 911, so many of the Normans who came from the south to invade England in 1066 were probably of Viking descent.

It's really not clear when the Viking Age officially ended. As with much of history, there was no one definitive moment or event that ended this period. Magnus Bare-Legs, who had become king of Norway, died in a raid in Ulster in 1103, but Viking raids in Wales continued into the 12th century. The Hebrides were still under Norwegian rule until 1266, Orkney until 1468 and Shetland until 1469.

The Battle of Stamford Bridge is considered to be one of England's greatest military victories, and it marked the last time a largely Scandinavian force would assault the island nation. After centuries of bloodshed and terror, what we think of as the Viking Age, which lasted more than 300 years, was at its end.

By this time, the Vikings had more or less converted to Christianity. All the Scandinavian kingdoms were Christian and the entire culture had begun to change.

Today, signs of the Viking legacy can be found mostly in the Scandinavian origins of the language in England, Scotland, Ireland, and Russia, and in the names of the areas where they made settlements. In Iceland, the Vikings left an extensive body of literature, collectively known as the Icelandic Sagas, in which they recall the finest victories of their magnificent past.

The pervading educational system that leans heavily on Greek and Roman mythology leaves the lore of the Vikings behind, but the Age of the Vikings is a thousand years closer to present day. As strange as some of their beliefs were, the richness of the culture should be remembered for what it was: one of exploration, war, creativity, and inspiration.

Chapter 13: Separating Viking Myths from Facts

There are a large number of myths and beliefs about the Vikings, many of which have come from the romantic heroic image of them portrayed in modern movies and paintings from the 19th century. The following list will clarify some of these myths and separate them from actual historical facts and archeological finds.

1. The Vikings did not wear horned or winged helmets.

The Vikings are often depicted wearing horned or winged helmets. There is no evidence, either historical or archeological, to support this, and this type of depiction may have come from the imaginations of artists who were inspired by the ancient Greeks and Romans. Norse, Celt and Germanic priests wore horned helmets for ceremonial and ritualistic purposes, and writers such as Plutarch mention northern warriors in horned and winged helmets, but that was several hundred years earlier, long before the Viking Age. Bronze Age (2500-800 BCE) and Iron Age (1200-550 BCE) helmets have been unearthed which have horns, but Viking battle helmets were typically bowl shaped and later bullet shaped with nose and cheek guards, and in some cases, were ornamented with carvings.

2. There were no women Viking warriors that we know of.

There were famous women, usually the wives of Viking warriors or Viking kings, who played some part in the development of their history, either by marrying into or across dynasties, killing their royal husbands, or supporting the cause of Christianity, but the image of the female Viking warrior with chain mail skirt and armor breastplate wearing a horned or winged helmet is not supported by history.

3. Most Vikings were not buried in their boats.

Viking boat burials were not common. This honor was reserved for the most valiant warriors and raiders, and for prominent people, including free women of high status. It was believed that the vessels that served these people in life would carry them into the afterlife and serve them there. They were surrounded by weapons, goods, sacrificed slaves and animals such as horses, oxen and dogs. Even if they were cremated (burned), they were still sent off with their weapons and valuable goods for the afterlife. Many artifacts unearthed from Viking burial sites include knives, axes, swords, ornate cups and drinking horns, pottery and other items, and although in many cases they're covered with rust, X-rays have shown them to be in extraordinary condition.

4. Vikings were not farmers.

In the true sense of the word, a Viking is a pirate, not a farmer, but most of the men and women who lived in the Viking Age in Viking settlements or communities were farmers. They were, therefore, not actual Viking pirates or warriors. The few hundred men from each village who went "viking" did so either part of the year or became part of the elite group who spent many months of the year raiding and exploring. These were career Vikings, some of whom became mercenaries.

5. Women had rights.

A free woman could inherit property, get a refund on her dowry if a marriage didn't work out, and could request a divorce. She could own thralls (slaves), have her own money, and generally marry whomever she chose when she was as young as 12 years old.

6. Vikings were slave traders.

As part of their plunder, Vikings would often take women and young men from Anglo-Saxon, Celtic and Slavic settlements, which they would then sell at large slave markets across Europe and the Middle East.

7. Viking culture had standards for hygiene.

It's a little hard to understand how these men could drive an axe through an enemies head, yet create laws that forbade them to throw dirt on someone to disgrace him, but that was what the *Grágás* (medieval Icelandic law book) stated. Severe penalties were inflicted on those who made someone dirty by pushing him into water or urine or food or dirt if the intent was to disgrace that person.

Archeologists have discovered wooden combs, metal tweezers, picks of bone, ivory or antler thought to be used to clean the teeth, and scrapers that would fit into the ear and so are thought to be ear cleaners. Items like these have been found at virtually every site that contained the remains of a body, whether male or female, and the conclusion is that they were commonly used in all Viking societies.

"Combed and washed, every thoughtful man should be, to ride to the Assembly though he may not be very well dressed; and fed in the morning, for one should not rush headlong before one's fate."

Hot spring baths built in the Norse era are still in existence today in modern Iceland, and a treaty negotiated in 907 between the Byzantine Empire and the Norse people of Sweden who traded with them stated that the Byzantines were obliged to provide them with baths as often as they wanted them.

8. People died younger in those days.

There are many skeletal remains that show people living into old age, up to 80 or more years, though they succumbed to joint degeneration, failing eyes and loss of hearing, the same old age maladies we suffer today. What differs, however, is that they did not suffer from diseases of stress, though one would think the battlefield to be the most stressful place. They showed no rampant signs of dental carries, but more tooth wear due to the coarse food. Even warriors lived and fought well into their fifties, if they managed to avoid the axe before that.

Appendix I: Who's Who in Viking History

Ælla: (mid-9th century) King of Northumbria who according to legend executed Ragnar Lothbrok. He was killed in 867 by Ivar the Boneless and the Great Heathen Army, supposedly as revenge for Ragnar's death.

Athelred the Unready: (c. 968 - 1016) King of England during the last great wave of Viking attacks.

Aethelwulf: (c. 795 - 858) King of Wessex and father of Alfred the Great.

Athelstan: (c. 894 - 939) First Anglo-Saxon monarch accepted as 'King of the English'.

Alcuin of York: (c. 735 - 804) English scholar who was one of the leading intellectuals of Charlemagne's court.

Alfred the Great: (c. 849 - 899) King of Wessex who defeated the Great Heathen Army. Laid the foundations of the medieval kingdom of England.

Aud the Deep Minded: (c. 834 - 900) Norwegian wife of the king of Dublin, Olaf the White, later settled in Iceland.

Basil the Bulgar-Slayer: (958 - 1025) Byzantine Emperor who founded the Varangian Guard.

Bjarni Herjólfsson (10th century) Norwegian explorer who first sighted mainland America.

Bjorn Ironside: (9th century) Son of Ragnar Lothbrok; In 860 he led a semi-legendary raid into the Mediterranean with his brother Hastein.

Brian Bóruma: (c. 941 - 1014) High King of Ireland who tried to unite the island under his rule. Killed at the battle of Clontarf.

Brodir of Man: (11th century) Danish Viking mercenary who according to legend killed Brian Bóruma at the battle of Clontarf.

Cnut the Great: (c. 985 - 1035) Viking king of England, Denmark, and parts of Norway. He was the son of Svein Forkbeard and conquered England from Athelred the Unready and his son Edmund Ironside.

Columba: (c. 521 - 597) Irish missionary credited with spreading Christianity in Scotland. The monastery he founded on the island of Iona in western Scotland became an early Viking target.

Cuthbert: (c. 634 - 687) Patron saint of northern England, his remains were kept at the monastery of Lindisfarne, target of the first major Viking raid.

Charlemagne: (c. 747 - 814) Frankish king and first monarch of the reborn Western Roman Empire.

Charles the Bald: (823 - 877) Frankish emperor, son of Louis the Pious. He confronted Ragnar at the first siege of Paris and bribed him to leave.

Charles the Fat: (839 - 888) Frankish emperor, great-grandson of Charlemagne. He was the last member of Charlemagne's dynasty to rule over a united empire.

Charles the Simple: (879 - 929) Frankish king, cousin of Charles the Fat. He attempted to stop Viking raids by allowing them to settle in Normandy.

Edmund Ironside: (c. 989 - 1016) King of England and son of Athelred the Unready. He agreed to divide England with the Viking king Cnut.

Erik Bloodaxe: (c. 885 - c. 955) Viking king of Norway and York, son of Harald Fairhair.

Erik the Red (Erik Thorvaldsson): (c. 950 - c. 1003) Norwegian Viking who colonized Greenland. Father of Leif Erikson and Freydis.

Freydis: (10th century) Daughter of Erik the Red; early colonizer of Vinland.

Garthar: (9th century) Swedish merchant who was the first Viking to deliberately sail to Iceland. He spent a single winter on the island.

Godfred: (late 8th century) Danish Viking warlord responsible for constructing the first sections of the Danevirke.

Godwin: (c. 1001 - 1053) Earl of Wessex, powerful advisor to Edward the Confessor and father of Tostig and Harold Godwinson.

Gorm the Old: (d. 958) First Viking king of Denmark, father of Harald Bluetooth.

Guthrum (d. 890) Leader of the Great Heathen Army during its invasion of Wessex.

Håkon the Good: (c. 920 - 961) Third king of Norway, youngest son of Harald Fairhair and brother of Erik Bloodaxe.

Halfdan: (d. 877) Son of Ragnar Lothbrok and one of the leaders of the Great Heathen Army. Briefly controlled London 871-2.

Harald Bluetooth: (c. 935 - 986) Viking king of Denmark and parts of Norway; Son of Gorm the Old, responsible for the Christian conversion of Denmark.

Harald Fairhair: (c. 850 - 932) First king of Norway, father of Erik Bloodaxe and Håkon the Good.

Harald Greycloak: (d. 970) Son of Erik Bloodaxe, king of Norway. Assassinated by Harald Bluetooth.

Harald Hårdrada: (c. 1015 - 1066) King of Norway and half-brother of Saint Olaf. Served in the Varangian Guard, conquered Norway, and died at the battle of Stamford Bridge.

Harald Klak: (c. 785 - c. 852) Danish Viking warlord that the Frankish emperor Louis the Pious attempted to use to Christianize Denmark.

Harold Godwinson: (c. 1022 - 1066) Last Anglo-Saxon king of England. Killed at the Battle of Hastings by William the Conqueror.

Hastein: (9th century) Possibly a son of Ragnar Lothbrok. Led a semi-legendary raid into the Mediterranean with his brother Bjorn Ironside.

Helgi: (d. 912) Swedish Viking who succeeded Rurik and moved the Rus capital from Novgorod to Kiev. Also known by the Slavic name Oleg.

Horik: (d. 854) Son of the Danish warlord Godfred, exiled Ragnar Lothbrok after the latter's raid on Paris.

Ingólfur Arnarson: (9th century) First permanent settler of Iceland. Settled and named Reykjavík.

Ingvar of Kiev: (d. 945) Swedish Viking who succeeded Helgi in Kiev. Led the Rus on an attack on Constantinople.

Ivar the Boneless: (9th century) Most famous son of Ragnar Lothbrok. Led the Great Heathen Army in a successful attack on England.

Leif Erikson: (c. 970 - c. 1020) Son of Erik the Red, first European to land in North America.

Louis the Pious (778 - 840) Frankish emperor, son of Charlemagne who unsuccessfully attempted to deal with Viking attacks on continental Europe.

Máel Sechnaill: (948 - 1022) ex High King of Ireland who reclaimed the title after Brian Bóruma's death at the battle of Clontarf.

Naddodd: (9th century) Viking explorer who is credited with discovering Iceland.

Odin: Chief of the Viking gods, known as the 'All-father'.

Olaf Haraldsson: (995 - 1030) Norway's patron saint. Viking king who attempted to Christianize Norway and was killed at the battle of Stiklestad. Half-brother of Harald Hardråda.

Olaf Sitricsson: (c. 927 - 981) Viking king of York and Dublin, son of Sitric One-Eyed.

Olaf the White: (c. 820 - 871) Viking king of Dublin; co-ruled with Ivar the Boneless.

Olaf Tryggvason: (c. 960 - 1000) Viking king of Norway, attempted to forcibly Christianize Norway and died at the battle of the Svold.

Olga of Kiev (c. 890 - 969) Regent of Kiev, wife of Ingvar of Kiev. Her acceptance of Christianity set the stage for the conversion of the Rus.

Ragnar Lothbrok: (9th century) Legendary Danish Viking. Led a successful raid on Paris in 845. Father of Ivar the Boneless, Hastien, Halfdan, Ubba, and Bjorn Ironside.

Raven Flóki: (9th century) Norwegian Viking who named Iceland and started its colonization.

Rollo: (9th century) Norwegian Viking who settled in France and allegedly founded Normandy through entitlement of land recognized by Charles the Simple, but there is little evidence to prove this.

Rurik the Rus: (d. 879) Swedish Viking who settled in Novgorod and founded the first Viking state in Russia.

Sigfred: (9th century) Viking warlord who led an unsuccessful siege of Paris in 885.

Sitric One-Eyed: (late 9th century) Viking king of Dublin and York, grandson of Ivar the Boneless. Attempted to create a Hiberno-English kingdom.

Sitric Silkbeard: (c. 970 - 1042) Viking king of Dublin. Last major Viking figure of Ireland. Started a revolt against the High King Brian Bóruma but withdrew before the battle of Clontarf.

Snorri Sturluson: (1179 - 1241) Icelandic poet who composed the Heimskringla, a history of the Norse Kings.

Sven Estridsson: (c. 1019 - 1074) Viking king of Denmark. Fought a fifteen year war with his neighbor Harald Hardråda.

Svein Forkbeard: (c. 960 - 1014) Viking king of Denmark, son of Harald Bluetooth. Conquered England in 1013.

Sviatoslav of Kiev: (c. 942 - 972) Ruler of Kiev, succeeded Ingvar. He was ambushed trying to cross the Dneiper River and his skull was made into a drinking cup.

Thor: Most popular of the Viking gods, especially with farmers and sailors.

Thorfinn Karlsefni: (11th century) Viking explorer who attempted a permanent settlement in Vinland.

Thorgils the Devil: (9th century) Viking sea-king who founded Dublin.

Thorvald Aswaldsson: Father of Erik the Red.

Thorvald Erikson: (9th century) Viking explorer, brother of Leif Erikson. Was the first European to be killed in the Americas.

Tostig Godwinson: (d. 1066) Brother of King Harold Godwinson, invited Harald Hardråda to attack England in 1066.

Ubba: (9th century) Son of Ragnar Lothbrok, one of the leaders of the Great Heathen Army.

Vladimir of Kiev: (c. 958 - 1015) Ruler of Kiev, converted the Rus to Christianity and provided the first Viking recruits to the Varangian Guard.

Glossary

Althing: Assembly of all free Viking men; summoned to vote on important decisions

Apples: The fruit symbolizes fertility, love and youth; the gods in Asgard eat apples.

Armagh Spiritual Center of Ireland: Burial place of St. Patrick.

Asgard: Home of the Aesir gods.

Bifrost: The Trembling Path; the rainbow bridge that connects Asgard and Midgard.

Brattahlíð: Erik the Red's farm in Greenland.

Clontarf: Most famous battle in Irish history, fought between the Irish High King Brian Bóruma and an alliance of Irish and Viking rebels.

Constantinople: Capital of the Byzantine Empire.

Danegeld: Bribes paid by English and Frankish kings to convince Vikings to leave their lands

Danelaw: Area of northern England originally held by Guthrum and settled by the Vikings.

Danevirke: Massive earthen wall extending along the neck of the Jutland peninsula to protect Denmark from Charlemagne's empire

Denmark: Southernmost Viking kingdom.

Dneiper River: Major Rus water route to Constantinople.

Dorestad: Important trading center of Charlemagne's empire; present day Wijk bij Duurstede in the Netherlands.

Dubgaill: 'Black Foreigners'; Irish name for Danish Vikings

Dublin: Most important city settled by the Vikings in Ireland.

Essex: One of the minor kingdoms of early Anglo-Saxon England. Controlled the land around London.

East Anglia: One of the major kingdoms of early Anglo-Saxon England. Located in the southeast of the island.

Eastern Settlement: First and largest colony started by Erik the Red in Greenland.

Fensalir: Fen Halls; home of the goddess Frigg.

Findgaill: 'White Foreigners'; Irish name for Norwegian Vikings

Frisia: Coastal region along the southeastern shores of the North Sea; present day Netherlands and Germany.

Gallgoidel: 'Foreign Irish'; Irish name for those with mixed Viking-Irish blood

Gothi: Icelandic elder respected for his reputation, knowledge of the law, generosity

Greek Fire: Byzantine secret incendiary weapon

Gimli: court of the gods after Ragnarok, with a roof made of gold.

Greenland: Largest island on earth, settled by the Vikings in the 10th century.

Hagia Sophia: Main cathedral of Byzantium and the Orthodox world.

Hebrides: Archipelago off the northwest coast of Scotland.

Hedeby: Most important trading center in the Danish peninsula; near present day Schleswig.

Heimskringla: History of the Norse Kings written by the Icelandic poet Snorri Sturluson

Hel/Helheim: Home of the dead and their ruler, the god Hel.

Iceland: Volcanic island in the North Atlantic just below the Arctic Circle; settled by the Vikings in the 9th century.

Idavoll: Plain of the last battle during Ragnarok.

Iona: Monastery on an island off the west coast of Scotland, founded by St. Columba.

Jarl: Viking noble

Kent: One of the minor kingdoms of early Anglo-Saxon England. Controlled the land around Canterbury.

Khazars: Powerful barbarian tribe controlling the Volga River access to the Caspian Sea

Kiev: Most important Rus city in the east; capital of first centralized state in Russia.

Land-Waster: Harald Hardråda's battle flag

Lindisfarne: Burial place of Cuthbert, patron saint of northern England; site of the first major Viking raid of note in 793, made off the coast of what is now north eastern England.

Longphort: Viking shore fortress which allowed them to winter in enemy territory

Mercia: One of the major kingdoms of early Anglo-Saxon England. Located in the center of the island.

Midgard: Middle Earth.

Miklagård: Viking name for Constantinople.

Northumbria: Northernmost of the seven kingdoms of early Anglo-Saxon England.

Norway: Westernmost Viking kingdom of the Scandinavian Peninsula.

Novgorod: First major city of the medieval Rus state.

Orkney: Islands Archipelago in northern Scotland southwest of the Shetlands.

Ragnarok: Mythical Last Battle where the gods would be overwhelmed by the ice giants

Raven Banner: This was the banner of Ragnar Lothbrok, woven in a single day by his daughters; he believed it carried the favor of Odin

Reykjavik: Capital of Iceland.

Setstokker: Inherited ornamented beams believed to be of significant mystical value.

Shetlands: Archipelago located roughly sixty miles north of Scotland.

Skræling: Viking name for the Natives populations of the North American continent

Stamford Bridge: Fought in 1066, it was the last major Viking battle and may have signaled the end of the Viking Age.

Staraya Ladoga: First outpost settled by the Rus.

Stiklestad: Fought between the exiled king Olaf Haraldsson and his former subjects.

Sussex: One of the minor kingdoms of early Anglo-Saxon England. Located on the Channel coast.

Sweden: Easternmost Viking kingdom of the Scandinavian Peninsula.

Thor's Hammer: A T-shaped amulet that resembles a hammer or Celtic cross, worn to invoke Thor's protection

Thrudheim: Home of the god Thor.

Treaty of St. Clair-sur-Epte: Agreement between King Charles the Simple and Rollo which created Normandy.

Valaskialf: Home of the god Odin.

Valhalla: Hall of the Slain located in Asgard where the 540 doors can walk 800 warriors side by side.

Varangian Guard: Name given to the Vikings by the Russians; Viking bodyguard of the emperors of Constantinople

Vinland: Viking name for the North American continent; most likely Newfoundland, Canada.

Volga River: Major Rus water route to the Caspian Sea and Islamic markets

Wessex: One of the major kingdoms of early Anglo-Saxon England. Located in the southwest of the island.

Western Settlement: Second Viking colony in Greenland; located northwest of the Eastern Settlement.

Yggdrasil: The Tree of Life located in Asgard. Its branches stretch over the Nine Worlds up the Heavens.

York: Major city of Northumbria; a center of Viking power in England

Other books available by author on Kindle, paperback and Audio

Greek Mythology: Greek Gods, Goddesses, Heroes, Heroines, Monsters, and Classic Greek Myths of All Time

Bibliography

The Völsunga Saga. Trans. Eirikr Magnusson and William M. Morris. London, Stockholm, New York: Noroena Society/Harvard College Library, 1906

Eirik's Saga Rauda (Saga of Erik the Red). Trans. J. Sephton, 1880

Nibelungenlied (The Song of the Nebelungs). Anonymous. Circa 1180

Beowulf. Unknown. Circa 700-1000

Dictionary of the Marine. William Falconer. London: Thomas Cadell, 1780

The Prose Edda. Sturluson, Snorre. Trans. Rasmus B. Anderson, LL.D. Chicago: Scott, Foresman and Company, 1901

The Prose Edda. Sturluson, Snorre. Trans. Brodeur, Arthur Gilchrist, Ph.D. London: Oxford University Press, 1916

Bella Parisiacae urbis. Abbo Saint-Germain-des-Prés. Trans. Nirmal Dass. Paris: Peeters, 2007

Konungs Skuggsjá. Unknown. Trans. Laurence Marcellus Larson. New York: The American Scandinavian foundation, 1917

Historia Norwegiæ. Anonymous. Trans. Peter Fisher. Copenhagen: Museum Tusculanum Press, 2003

Landnámabók. Unknown. Trans. Herman Pálsson and Paul Edwards. Canada: University of Manitoba Press, 2007

Annals of Ulster. Unknown. Trans. Sean Mac Airt and Gearoid Mac Niocaill. Dublin: Dublin Institute for Advanced Studies, 1983

Heimskringla. Sturleson, Snorri. Trans. Samuel Laing. London: Norœna Society, 1907

Orkneyinga Saga. Unknown. Trans. Jon Hjaltalin and Gilbert Goudie. Edinburgh: Edmonston & Douglas, 1873

The Viking Age Buildings of Dublin. Wallace, Patrick F. Dublin: Royal Irish Academy, 1992

Royal Irish Academy Dictionary. Dublin: Royal Irish Academy, 1981

The Viking Age. Byock, Jesse. London: Penguin, 2001

The Vikings. Ferguson, Robert. London: Penguin, 2009

Vikings: Raiders, Traders and Masters of the Sea. Castleden, Rodney. New York: Oxford Publishing, 2015

A History of the Viking Age. Carlson, Robert. 2015

The Sea Wolves: A History of the Vikings. Brownworth, Lars. Crux Publishing 2014

The Vikings: Conquering the Wind and Waves. Wernick, Robert. New Word City Press, 2014

The Vikings: Fury from the North. Wernick, Robert. New Word City Press, 2014

Vikings: History & Mythology. Weaver, Stephan. 2015

The Legend of Sigurd and Gudrún. Tolkien, J.R.R. Houghton Mifflin Harcourt, 2009.

Encyclopedia Britannica. Runic Alphabet. http://www.britannica.com/topic/runic-alphabet. Dec 2015

National Geographic. Nov. 2012. *Vikings and Native Americans.* Pringle, Heather. http://ngm.nationalgeographic.com/2012/11/vikings-and-indians/pringle-text Dec. 2015

20473352R00145

Printed in Great Britain
by Amazon